Warwick University Ltd
Industry, Management
and the Universities

Edited by E. P. Thompson

Spokesman

First published in 1970 by Penguin.
This edition published in 2014 by

Spokesman
Russell House
Bulwell Lane, Nottingham NG6 0BT, England
Phone 0115 9708318
Fax 0115 9420433
e-mail elfeuro@compuserve.com
www.spokesmanbooks.com

ISBN 978 85124 8295

A CIP catalogue record is available from the British Library

Printed by the Russell Press Ltd. (phone 0115 9784505)
www.russellpress.com

Wherever increasing stress is placed upon 'official secrecy', we take it as a symptom of either an intention of the rulers to tighten the reins of their rule or of a feeling on their part that their rule is being threatened.

Max Weber

Contents

Introduction to the New Edition

On February 3rd 1970, a student occupation of the Registry building took place at the University of Warwick, in protest at the authorities breaking a promise they had made to provide a student union building on the campus. As such, it was only one of many occupations that took place at British universities and colleges in the 1960s and 1970s, sometimes on issues of facilities as at Warwick; sometimes in pursuit of changes in teaching, management and research activities; and sometimes about wider social issues such as the Vietnam War. Unusually, however, the occupation at Warwick developed into a major public issue – the 'Warwick files affair' – with substantial national media coverage and legal repercussions well beyond the immediate issue at stake.

The reason for this was that in the course of a second occupation on February 11th, the students stumbled upon files in the Registry that provided clear evidence of the routine surveillance of staff and students, files that were kept apart from the normal information stored for administrative purposes. After much debate, selected documents were removed by the students, and their existence was reported to the historian E P Thompson, then Reader in Labour History at Warwick, and to the Student Union which had authorised the occupation. This led to the events recounted in Chapter 2 of the book, which came to involve the entire university through the following weeks, as well as newspapers, politicians and the courts.

While Warwick students and staff spread the news about the files and debated further action, E P Thompson published a passionate account of the background to the affair in the magazine *New Society,* which appeared on 19th February under the title 'The business university'. In it he linked the university's refusal to honour their promise of a union building not only to the political surveillance revealed in the files, but also to wider concerns about the origins, academic purpose and governance of the university. At that time, Penguin Books had established a form of instant book, which could present detailed investigative journalism on major issues in a convenient permanent form in a matter of weeks. Speedy negotiations with Penguin led to a contract to produce such a book – drafted in a week, edited in another week, and published in late March 1970, while the Warwick affair continued to hold the attention of the public.

The writing of *Warwick University Ltd* had an important effect on everyone involved. We learned a great deal not only about the origins and development of Warwick University, but also about the workings of business, the media, the judicial system, and the wider power structures of the UK within which these institutions function. For many of us, it gave impetus to our growing political awareness, setting us on our way to decades of activism in various forms, and providing us with experience in how to research and report on social issues.

Our purpose in republishing *Warwick University Ltd* is, however, not one of nostalgia. Rather, we believe that what our work revealed in 1970 is very relevant today; it represents an early milestone in the transformation of higher education, and our society as a whole, in the decades since then. The idea of republication took shape in January 2013, and the internet enabled us to put together a network of people involved in the Warwick events who warmly endorsed the project. Penguin Books declared that they had no objection to republication; leftwing publishers were approached, and advice sought from today's academic activists. We were surprised and pleased by the number of people we then came across who remembered what had happened at Warwick in February 1970, and recognised its relevance today.

In this introduction we try to do two things. First, we want to indicate the many ways in which what we uncovered at Warwick in 1970 prefigured the circumstances facing society today. It is a commonplace to see social change since 1970 in terms of the rise of a new individualism and a revival of liberal politics and free-market economics: the last forty years can all too easily be viewed as a time of retreat for socialism in any shape or form. So the first part outlines some of the common themes that link 1970 to the present day, both in higher education and in other areas of British social and political debate.

Second, despite the many defeats for the left since the 1970s, there have also been major social changes for the better, not only in increasingly tolerant attitudes towards alternative beliefs and life-styles, and the continued decline in deference towards our rulers, but also in the high politics of governments and world affairs, such as the end of apartheid and the formal restoration of democracy in many parts of the world. For a new generation of students, and for younger academics and interested citizens, we want to convey something of the personal and political context of that time. After a lot of discussion, and not a little disagreement, we decided that the best way of doing this was to present short personal sketches by three of our number who were all students at Warwick at the time: these make up the second part of what follows.

In the original edition of *Warwick University Ltd.*, individual authorship was only attributed for chapter 7, E P Thompson's closing 'personal comment'. This anonymity was partly due to the fear of legal action by the university authorities, which also restricted the general acknowledgement of contributors in the Preface; but it also reflected our commitment to a democratic and collective approach. For this new edition, we have tried to take a similar approach, but happily we no longer feel any threat of legal action. Accordingly, authorship of the new material is acknowledged: Hugo Radice wrote the first part on the links to the present, and acted as overall editor; the personal reflections are by Judith Condon, Ivor Gaber and Ron Rose; and Judith Condon prepared the index. Trevor Fisher has given unstinting support to the project throughout. We thank Barbara Winslow, Sol Picciotto, Julian Harber, Cal Winslow, Richard Hyman and Kate Thompson for their comments and advice. We also thank Cris Shore, Katrina Navickas, Andrew McGettigan, Andreas Bieler, Noel Castree, David Harvie, Massimo de Angelis, and Fred Lee from the wider higher education community for their encouragement; Peter Rous of the Print and Copy Bureau, University of Leeds, for technical assistance; Tony Zurbrugg of Merlin Press for his patience and generosity in discussing the publication of the new edition; and, finally, Tony Simpson of Spokesman Press who has brought the project to fruition.

Hugo Radice
October 2013

The relevance of *Warwick University Ltd* today

On June 20th 2013, echoing the events of 1970, an occupation took place at the University of Warwick. The Independent reported:

> 'A room of the Senate House building at the University of Warwick has been occupied by a group of students to protest against the "privatisation and marketisation" of higher education since late last week. The group calls itself Protect the Public University – Warwick (PPU) and has outlined eight "objectives", including that Vice Chancellor Nigel Thrift give up his £42,000 pay rise and use it to fund a bursary for local students.'[1]

Our immediate concern in writing *Warwick University Ltd* was to provide an explanation of the events of February-March 1970 at Warwick, and the analysis that we set out prefigures closely the travails of higher education today. We highlighted the contradictions in the liberal model of the university, based on a commitment to public service, academic independence, and close relations with local communities – all in the wider context of government policies and international scholarship. Local business interests had always played an important part in the establishment of the old civic and modern technological universities alike, as well as the polytechnics created in the 1960s, but within the rapid expansion that followed the 1963 Robbins Report, Warwick showed how this model could be moulded into a form that placed business at the heart of this constellation of interests. This shaped not only the academic development of the university, in terms of the balance of subject areas in teaching and research, but also the representation of external interests on the university's governing Council, and through that, its internal governance. In recent decades, higher education has become almost universally subordinated to commercial economic imperatives: these include the employability of students rather than their education as such; the provision of knowledge in the form of skills and research outputs of direct benefit to businesses and the state; and internal governance structures modelled on those of private companies. In addition, while universities have acquired more autonomy from central government, the decline in public funding has forced greater reliance on the 'markets' for both education and research, which have thus come to shape the choices made by university managers.

Beyond higher education, the occupation at Warwick also revealed the use of covert intelligence for political surveillance; the readiness of powerful interests to resort to the law when challenged; the subordination to the legal system of freedom of speech and of the media; and the readiness of supposedly respectable private businesses to defraud the state. In 1970, these issues were not widely perceived even by specialists in such matters, let alone the general public. In 2013, they stand at the centre of British politics, reflecting the wider processes of change from the post-war settlement that broadly prevailed from 1945 to 1979, towards what we now call neoliberalism.

The transformation of higher education

Chapter 1 of *Warwick University Ltd.* tells how the foundation of Warwick came to be hijacked by a secretive network of business, academic and political interests, marginalising the concerns of elected representatives and local communities. We explore the centralisation of administrative control under a small team of professional administrators, while the University Council was openly dominated by business interests, rather than a diversity of local representation; and we note how little voice academic staff – let alone students – had in major strategic decisions shaping the development of the university, and in its finances. Chapters 2 and 3 provide a detailed account of the events surrounding the occupation, and the disputes and decisions that led up to it; while Chapter 6, as well as reproducing the documents at the heart of the subsequent scandal, includes extracts from the 1968 Tyzack Report, with its recommendations for the 'streamlining' of university decision-making. These elements of what we termed 'the business university' closely prefigure the changes that swept the sector in the 1990s and after.[2]

The initial impact of the unrest at British universities during the heyday of the student movement – roughly 1968 to 1976 – was from our standpoint broadly positive. We welcomed the continuing expansion of higher education, because it challenged the traditional elitist concept of higher education. The movement won real gains in terms of opening up university management, with better representation and consultation for students, junior academics, and non-academic staff. We also succeeded in getting a broader curriculum in many subject areas, and innovation in teaching methods. Student unions ceased to be merely clubs providing social and sporting activities, and developed campaigning skills not only on issues of direct concern to students, but also on much wider issues of national and international politics.

By the end of the 1970s the picture had already darkened considerably. In 1976, the system of five-year grant allocations by the University Grants Committee (UGC), which had provided a degree of financial stability within which individual universities could plan their development, was abandoned as part of the Labour government's response to the severe fiscal constraints caused by runaway inflation, and by economic adjustment to the huge increase in oil prices in 1973-4. The return of the Tories under Mrs Thatcher in 1979 led to an even fiercer squeeze on credit and the public finances, and thereby to mass unemployment and deindustrialisation. This was accompanied by a sustained campaign against the labour movement, especially in the miners' strike of 1984-5; legislative assaults on workers' rights; the privatisation of public-sector utilities; the abandonment of remaining elements of corporatist indicative planning; the channelling of North Sea oil revenues into a revival of foreign investment by British capital; and later the deregulation of the financial sector.

In this context, higher education in the 1980s faced constant financial pressures, amid regular media attacks on both academic staff and management, with claims of waste and irrelevance. For the first time since the war, graduates faced worsening employment prospects, while academic workloads increased even as real pay stagnated. Nevertheless, the reforms of the 1970s largely persisted: academic governance remained more democratic than before, and both research and teaching more diverse. Within the university sector, the Association of University Teachers joined the Trades Union Congress (TUC), reflecting a shift from the model of a professional association to that of a trade union; while the expanding polytechnic sector attracted a more socially diverse intake and proved well able to generate high quality teaching and research.

The 1990s saw dramatic transformations in higher education in the UK: the abolition of the binary divide between universities (under the UGC) and polytechnics and teacher training colleges (mostly under local authority control); the introduction of central regulation and auditing of teaching and research, centred on Teaching Quality Audits and the Research Assessment Exercise (RAE); the subordination of academic planning to financial controls that extended down into academic departments and central services alike; continuous increases in workloads under the Orwellian rubric of 'efficiency gains'; and after the 1997 Dearing Report, the introduction of student fees and the replacement of grants with loans to cover living costs.

Such was the pace and scope of change that it took some time for staff and students across the sector to make sense of it all, let alone to appreciate the wider implications. While academic auditing probably improved the quality of teaching in many ways, it eventually led to a culture of box-ticking and gaming. As for research, while in principle the RAE led to greater transparency, it encouraged efforts by government to concentrate funding in élite institutions, and to many people it led to a culture of conformism.[3] With 'wealth creation' now openly seen as a crucial purpose of higher education, research became increasingly judged in terms of its impact on 'user communities', which in many fields meant primarily the business sector. Unions found it hard to resist the erosion of working conditions, and to negotiate the shift from academic to financial control systems.

By the turn of the century, New Labour's policy of expansion at first held out the prospect of improvements, at least for university staff, but instead it only revealed more clearly the extent of the changes, which were soon consolidated into the new-style neoliberal university that now prevails. While everyone knows about £9000-a-year tuition fees for undergraduates, new elements of marketisation have been less noticed, at least until recently: the spread of zero-hours contracts for part-time staff; the private financing of student residences; reductions in staff pensions and other benefits; outsourcing of many services; and the undermining of national collective bargaining.[4]

The university, business and the state

The wider relevance today of our analysis of the Warwick events centres first on issues relating to loyalty, surveillance and the law. To start with, the suspicion that members of the university community did not entirely support the policies of Warwick's leadership was a thread that connected the keeping of secret files, the language of the minutes of Council and Senate and the Tyzack Report, and the evidence of the narrow and carefully-managed 'representation' of academic staff in the higher reaches of decision-making. In this regard, the Warwick affair reached far beyond higher education, and here, too, the issues it raised have remarkable current resonance. The attempt to promote a particular concept of university education, and the general loyalty of staff and students, has its echoes today in the substantial investments by universities in image-building. This is often aimed at attracting private sector funding, as well as contributions from alumni, which provide senior management with financial resources not subject to direct state control. Access to such discretionary funds, disbursed through centralised corporate decisions, then functions as a means of securing consent within the organisation (see McGettigan 2013, ch.11).

If loyalty was desired, dissent within the university was undoubtedly feared. The documents uncovered in the Registry during the night of 11 February 1970 showed the lengths to which the University's senior managers, working with their business partners, the police and local politicians, would go to monitor and, if possible, suppress political dissent. It was one thing for politicians and pundits publicly to attack radical students and trade unionists who challenged the *status quo*, but quite another to mount covert surveillance, and to keep secret files whose existence was officially unrecorded.

In Chapter 4, we highlight the role of labour spies revealed by the correspondence concerning Professor David Montgomery's talk to Coventry Labour Party (March 1969) and the leafleting of an Automotive Products factory the previous month.[5] What we did not know was that 1968 had seen the formation within the Special Branch of the police service of the Special Demonstration Squad, the SDS,[6] which ever since has engaged in surveillance of political activism through police informers. We now know that the SDS later organised the infiltration of protest groups by dozens of undercover police officers, equipped with false identities, with some even fathering children with unsuspecting group members (see Evans & Lewis 2013).

We also found in the files documents from the Economic League reporting on two student groups, the Radical Students' Alliance and the Revolutionary Socialist Student Federation. We noted in Chapter 1 that the League was formed to foster the 'free enterprise spirit' and to oppose 'subversive forces', and that it was funded by businesses including several whose bosses sat on the University Council. The core of the League's work was the maintenance of a blacklist of left-wing trade unionists. Though it was formally closed down in 1993, the blacklist was thereafter secretly managed by a successor organisation, the Consulting Association, which was exposed only following a police raid on its premises in 2009. In August 2013 it was revealed that the Consulting Association had also been supplied with information on the political activities of trade unionists by 'embedded' police spies (*The Guardian*, 19 August 2013).[7]

What really made the Warwick files a matter for wide public debate was the University's immediate resort to the law, by obtaining an injunction to prevent the dissemination of the files. This too was a sign of things to come. The original interim injunction had been granted by an Assize judge in Birmingham on 12 February, and remained in force until 26 February, eight days after the *Birmingham Post* published extracts from the file documents. Chapter 5 gives an expert analysis of the enforcement of the injunction and the issues raised, highlighting the shaky legal foundations of the injunction procedure. We argued that, as a result, the University had to rely upon the general fear of legal action across the media, as well as on direct legal warnings to third parties, such as the printers of the York University student paper *Nouse*.

The use of the law to try to suppress dissent came into much sharper focus two years after Warwick, when the Shrewsbury Two, Ricky Tomlinson and Des Warren, were jailed for allegedly conspiring to organise an illegal picket during a strike of building workers. But the use of injunctions, as well as the effectively extra-legal D-Notice mechanism in matters of national security, has remained a significant factor in relation to the public expression of dissent ever since; indeed the law has developed so as to expand the reach of injunctions beyond those specifically identified in them. Most recently, on 25 March 2013, the University of Sussex resorted to an injunction against staff and students who were occupying a building in protest against the outsourcing of university services (*The Independent*, 27 March 2013).[8]

Equally, the media continue to play a central role in shaping the public perception of dissent. Particularly after the appearance of E P Thompson's *New Society* article on 19 February, the Warwick affair was clearly understood to raise questions of public interest, yet the main national newspapers refused to break ranks, relying on Press Council advice that owed much to the cosy relations between newspapers, the judicial system and politicians. There is a clear line of descent here from our experience in 1970 to the extraordinary tangle of illegality, intimidation and conformism exposed by the Leveson Inquiry, and the continued fierce resistance of the media to any form of regulation that entails transparency and democratic accountability.

The final element in the relation between the university and society at large concerns corruption within the relations between business and the state. To those of us opposed to the ever-wider subordination of higher education to commercial imperatives of financial markets and the demands of big business, Vice-Chancellors and their cheerleaders in the media always retort that we are thereby ignoring the 'realities' of the modern world, in which the livelihoods of our fellow citizens depend on the competitive success of the private sector. At Warwick, we found (see Chapter 1) that competitive success in the marketplace was, however, only one way in which big business could turn a profit. In the case of Bristol Siddeley Engines Ltd. (BSE), then a major aero-engine manufacturer, another method was to appropriate public funds through the deliberate manipulation of contracts to overhaul engines for the Ministry of Defence. The parliamentary enquiry into this had identified Sir Arnold Hall, who was the Pro-Chancellor of Warwick University in 1970, as one of those responsible.

Since then, business corruption has continued as a persistent feature of British public life, culminating most egregiously in the notorious Al-Yamamah deal covering the supply of jet fighters and other equipment by British Aerospace (later part of BAE

Systems) to Saudi Arabia. One of the ancestor companies of BAE was, of course, Bristol Siddeley Engines. All attempts to bring the company and its officials to justice have been thwarted, at the highest political levels. A more recent echo of the BSE case concerns two giant companies which have been given multiple contracts, worth billions of pounds a year, to supply public services. G4S and Serco are alleged to have systematically overcharged the Home Office for their contracts to tag offenders.[9] As in the BSE case, it is alleged that these firms charged for work not done, in this case by not reporting when tags were removed because offenders moved abroad, returned to prison, or died.

Conclusion

The wider context and implications of the Warwick affair come out most strongly in the final pages of E P Thompson's 'personal comment' (Chapter 7), and his analysis there remains extraordinarily relevant today. At its heart is the question of '... the whole way in which a society selects its priorities and orders itself'. The social order prevailing in Britain in 1970, he argued, was one in which everything was subordinated to the needs of the industrial and business system, and thus to the managers and financiers who ran it. Ostensibly, the system aimed at efficiency and economic growth; in reality it was guided by profitability, and imposed by the subjugation of individuals to its institutions. He insisted that the problem was not just the measures taken to enforce this order on reluctant subordinates, but the 'whole system of values'. If these values became accepted, then the allegiance of the scholar would shift from 'a national or international discourse of ideas' to the inexorable dictates of the existing social order: 'In his submission to a subordinate role in a managerial system, he is re-enacting the meaning, in Britain in the 1970s, of the *trahison des clercs*'.

In 2013 Britain, this reference needs some explanation. *Le trahison des clercs* – translated as *'The Betrayal of the Intellectuals'* – was a 1927 polemic by the French writer-philosopher Julien Benda, in which he argued that intellectuals were betraying their commitment to knowledge and truth by declaring allegiance to specific ideologies and political systems. Today, with the rise and rise of endowed chairs and research centres, the commitment is more mundane and often crudely financial: examples include the acceptance of funding from the Gaddafi régime in Libya by the London School of Economics and the funding of research by tobacco and pharmaceutical firms.

Nevertheless, the ever-increasing subordination of scholarship to commercial goals and values has met continuing resistance. Students campaigned strongly against the introduction of fees, and even more so, in 2012, against their increase up to £9,000 a year, while also providing much of the wider resistance to neoliberalism through the Occupy movement and UK Uncut. Academics have established campaigning groups such as the Campaign for the Public University and the Council for the Defence of British Universities.[10] It is also important to recognise that the refashioning of higher education under neoliberalism has been taking place not just in the UK, but all over the world, highlighting the need to co-ordinate resistance internationally.[11]

Warwick University Ltd. is relevant not only in providing useful historical background to the travails of higher education and society today, but also in offering a basis for an alternative. Underlying our purpose in writing the book was our heartfelt belief that we could rebuild the university on a different model, one based on community engagement and democratic values, rather than economic motives and managerial efficiency. In the closing section of Chapter 7, E P Thompson set out this vision with eloquence and passion, and his words provide an invaluable starting-point for us all today.

Hugo Radice

* * *

Warwick in 1970

Judith Condon

We were, as we know now, the favoured segment of a very fortunate generation. Arriving at Warwick in autumn 1968, simply attending university was as far ahead as I could see. The literature syllabus was modern and broad in scope. The buildings – white tiled and far flung – were not traditional and oppressive, and many of the academic staff were young, even hip.

The new universities of the '60s created breathing space amidst the dusty, churchy culture of Oxbridge, Durham and the like. The Victorian red bricks had their own imposing buildings and values

– I'd already had a bewildering false start in one of those. But the new universities sat geographically and culturally apart – a fresh start. At the time of the events described in this book, Warwick was small enough for students to meet and debate every day across faculty lines and political tendencies.

Who were we? Typically, the product of single-sex grammar schools and the first in our families to enter higher education. For us state support and social progress went hand in hand. We'd seen the Beatles conquer America and England win the World Cup. Working class was cool and you could go just about anywhere by sticking out your thumb on the M1. I don't forget the anxiety, the cold damp house in Kenilworth, and all-round existential angst. But at the campus surgery Dr Paine (how could one forget the name?) would prescribe The Pill if you really convinced him, and that, too, was progress: the contraceptive pill at this time was generally only made available to married women.

In this novel environment, we had no idea that the university's governance and structures had been forged in the image of manufacturing industry and under the influence of some of its captains; nor how opposed they were to the very notion of a students' union.

Our world was political, progressive, international. The word 'student', usually preceded by 'long-haired', seemed anchored to the word 'protest'. In the spring of 1968, mass protest by students and workers had shaken the government in France, and later in Czechoslovakia the rise of a new generation had been suppressed by Russian tanks. How lucky we were that Harold Wilson kept the UK from being sucked into Vietnam – but now that war came into our lives nightly via television news. The same year saw two huge anti-war demonstrations in London, and an active movement of young Americans to resist the draft. Barclays, the only bank on campus at Warwick, was boycotted for its involvement in apartheid South Africa. The Springboks tour was stalked and disrupted. Like most of my friends, I joined demonstrations that were at once empowering and frightening. It was not a time to sit on the fence.

The events at Warwick had unique features, but they were of their time. The fact that there was an annual exchange of history students with the United States made for a cross fertilisation of radical ideas. US students got to meet British socialists and trade unionists (Coventry being a powerful centre of union activism). British students got to meet Americans who had joined the march on the Pentagon, the Berkeley Free Speech Movement, the freedom marches, and the nascent women's movement. (Which male member of staff was quoted as saying 'women at university are sexual cannon fodder'?) The first national women's liberation conference was in Oxford on the last weekend of February 1970 – the same month as the occupation – while Germaine Greer, then a lecturer at Warwick, was drafting *The Female Eunuch*.

It's striking to recall how readily and rapidly students mobilized – no internet, no mobile phones. Distributing documents meant lots of typing and the churning of a duplicator. But we had sufficient political nous to hold the high ground, plus the energy to stay up all night. In the heady days described here we learned fast too: crucially that knowledge is power.

Personally, I remember in particular: the sense that if students stuck together in common purpose – on one occasion 'rough musicking' the university council from outside as the only way to make our voice heard – then the authorities could not ignore us; the exhilarating moment after the files were uncovered, when we spread out to our departments and debated what their contents meant for the notion of academic freedom; the unhesitating leadership of E P Thompson, who published first to the academic community at Warwick and then, via Penguin, to anyone willing to know; and the courage of Professor Epstein when he spoke out on 16 February, bringing the house down in more ways than one.

For the record, I was named on the injunction though as far as I remember I was not in the registry building at the time it was delivered by loud-hailer. And it absolutely wasn't Annie or Julian or I who gave out leaflets outside the school in Kenilworth. History as reported by informants and recorded in documents is to be treated as critically as history recounted by participants. I hope new readers of this book will read it all, therefore, and come to their own conclusions about the relevance of what came to light then to what happened subsequently.

An atmospheric footnote, because the personal, after all, is political: in picturing the scenes described here you need to add smoke. People smoked – routinely – in the bar, in seminars, in meetings. As a non-smoker I spent a lot of my time at university coughing. Also, by far the majority of players – students, lecturers and, of course, Council – were male, and even more overwhelmingly were white.

* * *

Ivor Gaber

Memory's a funny thing. Events that you are sure that you witnessed turn out to be 'memories' that you heard about or read about but have repeated often enough so that they take on a reality of their own. Hence, any 'remembering' of the events surrounding *Warwick University Ltd*, 40 years on, come with a health warning.

But to begin with what is not memory. In talking to my Warwick friends and acquaintances over the years I encounter a real bifurcation. There are those, like me, who found the whole experience enjoyable (more later) and yet I also encounter those who describe the Warwick years as among the unhappiest of their lives. I am not going to attempt any cod historical psychology, but merely observe that these varying memories of mood play an important part in how we reflect on the specific events leading up to what happened in 1970.

I was lucky in that, before I arrived at Warwick, I had spent what for me was a miserable year at the LSE. I was living at home, commuting into work, studying a subject I found boring in an institution that was surprisingly conservative. Warwick was a breath of fresh air, I was away from home, I didn't find the campus an alienating environment, I loved my subjects, and I was continually impressed by the willingness of staff to discuss with us course content and structure – and even to accept some of our suggested changes.

Then there was politics. The Warwick 'Soc Soc' (Socialist Society), where I spent most of my political 'leisure time', was a melting pot of ideas. Despite the preponderance of International Socialists, there were others who came from a wide variety of left groups, excluding the Labour Party – I cannot recall a single member of the Party (where I have spent the last 40 years of my life) ever making an appearance at a Soc Soc meeting. I was a political independent then – still am really – but allowed myself to be signed up to the Revolutionary Socialist Students Federation (with the subsequent unintended effect of finding myself banned from the US and the BBC within 12 months of leaving Warwick).

We students hated Rootes Hall, but we also loved it. It wasn't a students' union building, and we had no say in its running; the main barman was an unpleasant (probably racist) tyrant. But it was the centre of many of our lives (apart from the pubs of Leamington). Before the days of mobile phones, Facebook and Twitter, we had our own 'social media' – the top of the stairs at Rootes Hall, where almost everybody passed by during the day. And in the evenings it was where we drank, talked and flirted – and not just students, young staff also lingered and socialised.

Warwick University Ltd gives the impression that Warwick was a politically somnambulant place with student and political apathy the dominant motif. That is not how I recall it (though I have to say the experience of working in current British universities makes virtually all universities in the 1960s appear to be veritable cauldrons of political activity.) For me at least, in the months and years leading up to the events described here, Warwick was a highly political place. Maybe the presidency of the students' union was of little concern, and the Students' Representative Council seemed irrelevant, but attendance at demonstrations – local and national – against apartheid, the Vietnam War and other causes was not an infrequent event. I recall intense discussions within Soc Soc about a range of issues – including what must have been among the first stirrings of the new wave of feminism on a British campus – that make inappropriate notions of political apathy and isolation. I also recall meetings with Coventry shop stewards and leafleting in the shopping centre, all of which meant that, when the events of early 1970s began to unfold, there were sufficient numbers of students around with a knowledge of activism and a political narrative to make what happened, if not inevitable, at least not surprising.

That brings me to what I believe to be the central 'truth' of the events and of the *Warwick University Ltd* account – the recognition that there was a malaise at the heart of the University, in terms of the influence of outside corporate interests in directing both the University's long-term trajectory and also, perhaps surprisingly, some of its day-to-day management. In taking the action we did we might have weakened the control of the industrialists at Warwick, but we failed to halt the long-term attack on the independence of British universities which has come to dominate much of current academic life.

So much for the negative. I think that there were two positives, at least, to be drawn from these events. The first was that, according to Professor Epstein (who spoke at an event Trevor Fisher helped organise at Warwick a few years back), we students by our actions gave the academics the confidence to take back some of the powers that the Council, dominated by lay interests, had taken over. This led to the creation of a more balanced Warwick where, along with its continuing relations with business and industry, there developed a very strong core of more traditional academic subjects, resulting in the development of the academically successful institution we see today. And second, even though we never achieved a joint staff/student social building, there is now a large and student-controlled students' union building which, but for our efforts, might never have taken shape.

I was one of those lucky enough to be taught by E P Thompson at Warwick; it was a course called 'Politics and Poetry' and I've always remembered the lines from Wordsworth's 'The Prelude' about the French Revolution – lines which Edward so enthused about – for they encapsulated my own Warwick experience. Wordsworth wrote,

Bliss was it in that dawn to be alive,
But to be young was very heaven.

One final memory – and this one I know to be real. During the events of 1970 I was at a party in Coventry chatting with a Soc Soc member (and a former Students' Union President). Perhaps slightly the worse for having ingested too much cheap wine, we were musing on the unfolding events: 'You realise we're taking on capitalism?' said Dave, without any apparent sense of irony. Equally seriously I replied, 'Yes, I know'. In retrospect it appears to me that, irony aside, we were. The only problem was that, in the long term, we lost!

* * *

Ron Rose:
I was the first member of my family to go to University. I chose Warwick because it was the only university English Literature course in the country that did not have O-level Latin as a condition of entry.

My A-level results were crap. But I had been interviewed by

George Hunter, the Glaswegian professor, and he must have liked me because he wrote and said they were oversubscribed but if I still wanted a place the next year, get in touch. I did, and there was.

I was northern working class. My dad drove a meat delivery van for the Co-op. He voted Conservative. It was so cold at home I once set my pyjamas on fire trying to read by candlelight. My grant was twelve quid a week. Paid to sit in a warm library reading books. My dad got eleven for a 48-hour week. I'd gone to the TUC while competing in the National Swimming Championships at Blackpool, and heard Clive Jenkins and others talk about low pay, and made the connection that had eluded the rest of my family.

There were posh kids at Warwick with weird accents. One lad was so strangulated that I followed him around for days waiting for the pretence to slip. It didn't. He really was like that.

Hunter's ferocious introductory lecture informed us that, whatever illusions we might be entertaining, we were there to work. My personal tutor was Germaine Greer. My mum had not prepared me for that. My consciousness desperately needed raising and embarked on a steep and rapid learning curve.

Politics was conducted by people who talked about the working classes with an 'r' in it; a 'class' we Northerners did not recognise. And for the first and probably the last time there were quite a lot of us at Warwick.

Comparatively unsophisticated, we nevertheless arrived on the back of sixties cultural influences: of television satire; of American music protest – Dylan and all the rest; of emerging investigating journalists and Private Eye. Viscerally, if we were leaned on, our generation leaned back.

The strength of the Warwick Files protest was that it involved the overwhelming majority of the students. The most surprising people turned up every night to meetings. At the next graduation, only a handful of English graduates collected their degree after a departmental vote in favour of a boycott.

What we experienced during the Files Affair was an education about how the world works. Subsequently, a significant proportion of us became writers, journalists, teachers. The awkward squad. The grit in the machine. We didn't halt Capitalism, but we did irritate it. We reminded them that we were here. Many of us still do.

I couldn't have contemplated the level of debt you need to take on to get a degree now. And the boy I was then would have found the current social mix at Warwick very uncomfortable.

You win small battles. Some not so small. There were no women on the Committee of Seven: wouldn't happen now. Universities are ranked in order of academic excellence. The struggle continues.

E P Thompson wrote in a letter some years later: 'It's good that so many of that Warwick period remain politically active and sane.' Active, anyway.

Notes

1 See http://www.independent.co.uk/student/news/warwick-university-buildings-occupied-in-privatisation-protest-8667161.html.

2 For a fuller account of developments between 1970 and the present, see Radice (2013). Current issues in the funding and management of UK universities are fully examined in McGettigan (2013).

3 The funding and management of research is discussed in Gillies (2008).

4 For detailed analysis of recent trends and their implications see Barber, Donnelly and Rizvi (2013).

5 For more on David Montgomery, see http://www.theguardian.com/books/2011/dec/11/david-montgomery.

6 Did they deliberately choose this acronym to echo the US student organisation, Students for a Democratic Society? And were they covertly present in the Warwick struggle?

7 See http://www.theguardian.com/uk-news/2013/aug/18/police-activists-blacklisting-agency-alleged.

8 See http://www.independent.co.uk/student/news/university-of-sussex-granted-injunction-against-student-occupation-8551231.html.

9 See http://www.theguardian.com/business/2013/jul/11/g4s-investigated-overcharging-millions-pounds.

10 See http://publicuniversity.org.uk/ and http://cdbu.org.uk/.

11 Useful blogs covering developments around the world include http://universitypolitics.blogspot.co.uk and http://www.isa-sociology.org/universities-in-crisis.

References

Michael Barber, Katelyn Donnelly and Saad Rizvi, *An Avalanche is Coming: Higher Education and the Revolution Ahead*, Institute for Public Policy and Research, March 2013 (available at http://www.ippr.org/publication/55/10432/an-avalanche-is-coming-higher-education-and-the-revolution-ahead).

Julien Benda, *The Betrayal of the Intellectuals* (with an introduction by Herbert Read), Beacon Press, Boston, 1955.

Rob Evans and Paul Lewis, *Undercover: the True Story of Britain's Secret Police*, Faber & Faber, London, 2013.

Donald Gillies, *How Should Research be Organised*, College Publications, London, 2008.

Andrew McGettigan, *The Great University Gamble: Money, Markets and the Future of Higher Education*, Pluto Press, London, 2013.

Hugo Radice, 'How we got here: UK higher education under neoliberalism', *ACME: An International E-Journal for Critical Geographies*, vol.12 no.3, 2013; see http://www.acme-journal.org/Home.html.

E P Thompson, 'The business university', *New Society*, 19 February 1970, pp 301-4.

Notes on the contributors

Hugo Radice did an MA in Economics at Warwick in 1968-69, and became involved in the Warwick events as a reporter for a radical student paper. He worked in higher education, eventually teaching economics and politics at the University of Leeds from 1978 to 2008. He continues to research and write on contemporary capitalism from a socialist standpoint.

In February 1970, *Judith Condon* was a second year undergraduate studying English. She is currently associate director of a national information service for school leaders and governors, having previously worked for the Workers' Educational Association and the Open University. Her books for young readers range from recycling to Chernobyl and other nuclear accidents.

In 1970 *Ivor Gaber* was coming to the end of his undergraduate degree in History and Politics. He began his career as a journalist covering politics for radio and TV. He then moved into academia and currently holds posts at City University London and the University of Bedfordshire where he teaches and researches politics and the media – about which he has written extensively.

At the time of the Files, *Ron Rose* was a third year undergraduate reading English and American Literature. He is a professional scriptwriter with many television, stage and radio credits. He was the whistleblower in the Donnygate local government scandal which resulted in more than 80 arrests, with consequent prison sentences, fines and bans.

Preface

This book, which was written in a week, is the combined effort of a group of staff and students at Warwick University – David Fallows, Fred Clarke, Douglas Hay, Hugo Radice (graduate student 1968–9), Peter Mottershead, Ivor Gaber, Luke Hodgkin, Richard Hyman, Sol Picciotto, Paul Davies and myself. Advice and information was given by many other colleagues, in particular Professor David Epstein and members of the elected 'Committee of Seven'. We were also helped in numerous ways by Councillors (and, in particular, by Alderman G. E. Hodgkinson) and others involved in the foundation of Warwick University. We would also like to acknowledge the help of the Labour Research Department.

Although individuals were responsible for particular sections many editorial amendments were made at a late stage to most pieces, and these are my final responsibility. The work would have been impossible without the active editorial assistance first of Hugo Radice and then of several long-suffering and extremely efficient Penguins. Robert Hutchison settled at Warwick for a week, and acted throughout as my associate editor; Marian Newbold and Jonathan Croall worked late into the night to reduce the copy to order, and to prepare it for the printer.

Some parts of *Warwick University Ltd* grew out of my article, 'Warwick: The Business University', published in *New Society* on 19 February 1970.

Finally, we are grateful to *The Times* and the *Birmingham Post* for their permission to report the former's third leader of 21 February 1970, and the latter's 'Comment' column of 24 February 1970.

E. P. Thompson
Warwick
20 March 1970

The Power Structure at Warwick University[1]

Council
Chancellor: Viscount Radcliffe
Pro-Chancellor and Chairman of Council: Sir Arnold Hall
   (Hawker Siddeley)
Vice-Chancellor: John B. Butterworth
Pro-Vice-Chancellor: Professor W. Harrison
Treasurer: R. J. Kerr-Muir (Courtaulds)
6 local councillors (3 Warwickshire, 3 Coventry)[2]
2 Academic Advisory Committee nominees[3]
8 Senate representatives
9 co-opted members (8 businessmen and the Bishop of
   Coventry)[4]

Finance and General Purposes Committee
Chairman:
   R. J. Kerr-Muir
Vice-Chancellor
Pro-Vice-Chancellor
2 co-opted members
   (A. F. Tuke – Barclays,
   J. F. Mead)
2 academics
   (Professor V. M. Clark,
   Dr A. G. Ford)

Building Committee

Chairman: Gilbert Hunt
   (Rootes)
Vice-Chancellor
Pro-Vice-Chancellor
2 co-opted members (Sir
   R. D. Young – Alfred
   Herbert, Sir W. Lyons –
   British Leyland)
1 local councillor
2 academics
   (Professor H. A. Clegg,
   Dr A. H. T. Levi)

Senate
Chairman: Vice-Chancellor
Pro-Vice-Chancellor
Librarian
3 Deputy Chairmen of the Boards of Studies[5]
4 Board of Arts appointees
4 Board of Sciences appointees
4 Board of Social Studies appointees
6 academics elected by Assembly
2 professors elected by the Professorial Board

Estimates and Grants Committee
Chairman:
  Vice-Chancellor
Pro-Vice-Chancellor
Deputy Chairmen of
  Boards
Professor G. K. Hunter
Professor J. M. Buxton

1. For a discussion of the workings of the system, see 'The Union Building Saga' (p. 60).
2. All Conservatives at present.
3. Due to lapse in May 1970, and to be replaced by Senate representatives. (In fact, for obscure reasons, one AAC place has already been filled by a Senator – Professor V. M. Clark – nominated *not* through Senate but through Council.)
4. See 'The World of Industry' (p. 31).
5. Under the University statutes the Vice-Chancellor is *ex officio* Chairman of all Boards of Studies.

Chapter 1
The Business University

Introduction

The first Chancellor-designate of the new University of Warwick was the first Lord Rootes of Rootes Motors Ltd. After his death in 1964 the first students' hall was officially named after him: Rootes Hall. The second Lord Rootes and the Managing Director of Rootes Motors, Mr Gilbert Hunt, took places on the University's governing Council. Mr Hunt was not an inactive member of this Council. As Chairman of its crucial Building Committee he was able to influence policies and priorities in relation to some millions of pounds of capital expenditure (by far the greater part being public – Treasury – money) – which buildings, in which order, which architects. For three years the Building Committee resisted a series of hard-pressed demands from the students, and also from academic staff, whose objectives were to humanize the starkly utilitarian social environment, to desegregate the informal life of students and staff, and to afford to the students this or that measure of control over their own union building. Finally, on 11 February 1970, one more prevarication by the Building Committee on the issue of student control precipitated an occupation of the Registry.

A good deal was unveiled there, some of which filtered through to the outside world – despite a legal injunction – in the next two or three weeks. This is one of the themes of this book. It turned out, for example, that Mr Gilbert Hunt had not confined his active interest in university affairs to the problems of building and of student social life. He had been so kind as to employ the services of the Legal Adviser of the Rootes Organization, Mr N. P. Catchpole, of an industrial 'security officer' and of a shorthand writer, to report on the political activities of a distinguished visiting American professor (perhaps with a view to criminal or deportation proceedings?) and to send on the reports to the Vice-Chancellor 'for your confidential files'. He had also been sending information to the Vice-Chancellor, at his private address, upon the political activities of at least one other lecturer.*

Mr Hunt himself was busy in the next week or two since he was doing some unveiling on his own account – of the new Hillman Avenger. It is – wrote the ecstatic motoring correspondent of the *Sunday Express*, Robert Glenton – 'a car for all ages, suitable to be parked outside a discotheque or the town hall'. More than £400,000 was spent by Rootes on promotion and publicity: a jamboree for sales executives and correspondents in Malta, Avenger girls in black leather gear. The Avenger Grand Luxe could come with options – a Luxury, Pathfinder or Personality pack, or an exclusively styled cigar lighter for the top executive. The hard-spined, streamlined form of business efficiency – greater productivity, cost-analysis, the drive for exports – turned over for a moment in the choppy seas of competitive commerce, and revealed its soft white underbelly – swinging 'classless' hedonism, conspicuous sexual display, and an open celebration of money and of success which would have shocked the nonconformist mill-owners and the ascetic Quaker bankers of the first Industrial Revolution. (For this also – one must insist – this glamour of cash and success, this growing style of highly fee'd lecture tours to the United States, of assent to the glamour of Mediterranean conferences, television fees and industrial consultancies – is one way in which close relations with 'industry' can find expression within a university's walls.) Meanwhile, Chrysler International, the new parent of Rootes, was watching the operation quizzically, anxious about throwing good money after bad. 'Rootes must become really profitable as quickly as possible,' said Mr Hunt. 'One thing is sure,' said Mr Glenton in the *Sunday Ex-*

---

* See page 110. It must be stressed that we have at Warwick no means of establishing the extent of this political surveillance of students and of staff, since the file in which most of this came to light was in the Vice-Chancellor's area of the Registry; and, early in the occupation, other files were removed from this area. Circumstances suggest that the most obnoxious file may have been left behind by an oversight.

press: 'Rootes have gambled millions, their shirts, socks, grandmother's boa and all their prospects, on its doing so.'

The students had only gambled their academic careers. Even their grandmothers' ostrich plumes were unlikely to stand up against the Avenger Mark II which (it was more than probable) the Finance and General Purposes Committee of the University's Council would unveil in the wake of the injunction. They appealed to public opinion.

Public opinion came up: but only just. The breakthrough came in two areas. First, in areas where the journalist's profession is still respected, the sweeping character of the injunctions provoked the suspicion that someone had something to hide: the *Guardian* and the *Sunday Times* broke surface with important stories. The editor of *New Society* faced a confrontation at law with the University by publishing the article on 'Warwick: The Business University'. And the editor of the *Birmingham Post* simply put down his head and walked through the legal ambiguities of the injunction day after day.

The second area was that of the socialist press. The *Morning Star* was the first national paper to publish the Montgomery documents, and support came quickly from *Tribune*, the *Socialist Worker*, and the socialist and student underground. Here the lightning and very efficient counter-espionage movement of some of the students, in editing and duplicating a selection of documents and in circulating them – not only at Warwick, but in a number of other universities – was the critical factor. Within two weeks a wave of sympathy movement broke out at a dozen other universities.

The preparation of this book for the press is also a lightning operation. It has been put together swiftly by a group of Warwick students and staff, many of whom have been and continue to be deeply involved in the events described. As we write the outcome of these events is still unclear. We would have liked to have pursued our researches further in this and in that direction. We are well aware that we should have done some of this research long before.

In one sense this analysis concerns a specific situation, and one peculiar to Warwick. For example, the files that revealed the objectionable material were not the general student record files of the Registry but the files held in the Vice-Chancellor's area, to which only a few confidential secretaries had access. The Vice-Chancellor's style of operation, the Tyzack Report, the apparent attempt to limit democratic processes and to ensure the loyalty of administrators and staff, the peculiarly subordinate relationship with 'industry' – and the degree of power exerted by a few industrialists on the University's Council – all these may indicate a situation in Warwick which is, in some ways, unique. And, in this sense, it would be wrong not to see Jack Butterworth, and the house that he built, as a self-contained episode. We try to present this episode as cogently as we can, without going into a hundred and one details of in-fighting and of petty academic conspiracy.

In another sense this analysis points towards a general situation, to the operative modes of power and of money in Britain in 1970, and to the relationship of our institutions of higher education to industrial capitalism. The poetic logic by which Mr Gilbert Hunt, Managing Director of Rootes, was simultaneously Chairman of the Building Committee (whose policies provoked the occupation) and author of political surveillance of academic staff, is too neat. He is only one of a group of industrialists whose influence upon the University's life have been felt in pervasive, if less sensational, ways. Nor can the malaise of Warwick be diagnosed in the single personality of its Vice-Chancellor. His policies of ever closer relationships with 'industry' have been staunchly supported at different times by government, by the University Grants Committee, and by Science and Social Science Research Councils, as well as by the industrialists on his Council. And a good part of these policies has been readily assented to by leading members of his academic staff, whose departments have derived from them substantial benefits.

In this sense the case of Warwick no longer appears as unique. How far it is a paradigm or prototype of other places, how far it points towards tendencies only beginning to reveal themselves elsewhere – this is for our readers to decide and, by their own researches, to find out.

It is sobering to realize that the Mid-Atlantic of the Midlands Motor and Aircraft Industry offers one possible model of a British future. It is a febrile, wasteful, publicity-conscious world, whose prosperity floats upon hire-purchase and the shifting moods of the status-conscious consumer; a brash, amoral, pushful world of expense-account living, lavish salesmanship, cocktail bars in restored sixteenth-century inglenooks, and of refined managerial techniques and measured day-work; a world of mergers and take-overs, of the unregenerate, uninhibited Mammon of the Sunday business supplements; a world in which more than £3½ million of excess profits can be pocketed from the taxpayer (in part by double-charging on the same contracts), so that even some of the workers on the shop-floor admire the management for getting away with it for so long.

Presiding over this world are some of the new lords of this country. Just as the great landed aristocracy of the eighteenth century exerted their power by manifold exercise of interest, influence and purchase, so the new lords seem to infiltrate the command-posts of our society, including our educational institutions, not through any transparent democratic process, but quietly, in unnoticed ways. They apparently share with their precursors the same assumption that this is *their* world, to dispose of by ownership and by right of purchase. These are the people who know other people; who govern by telephone; who are unaccountable because it is always their inferiors who make up the accounts; who put things in each others' laps.

It was this world which the students of Warwick found themselves suddenly confronting on the night of 11 February; in the next week, as we struggled to break through to public opinion, we were nose-to-nose not only with Rootes but with directors of Courtaulds, Hawker Siddeley and Barclays Bank. In the conflict it became apparent that what was wrong was not a close relationship with 'industry' but a particular kind of subordinate relationship with industrial capitalism – with an industrial capitalism, moreover, which exerts its influence not only directly in the councils of the University but also within the educational organs of the State, and which, from both directions, is demanding, for its better service, an approved educational product.

But, at the same time, it became apparent that this seemingly neutral word, 'industry', was itself the great illusion. To dispense with industry would be to dispense with the very means of life. Industry is more than managing directors, and industrial consultancies for professorial staff. It is also workers and technicians and the organizations of the labour movement. The workers at the Rootes factories in Coventry no more welcomed the attentions of Mr Gilbert Hunt and Mr Catchpole than did the students and staff of the University. It became clear that the conflict which had opened on 11 February could not end with the replacement of this or that officer of the University: its logic demanded the radical restructuring, not only of the University's internal government, but also of the relationship between the University and the people of the West Midlands.

The Foundation

When examining the early moves towards establishing the University of Warwick, one is soon struck by the vision and enthusiasm of Coventry City Council. After the Second World War their city was going to be rebuilt, and they wanted to have as much pride in what they created as they had had in the beautiful medieval town that had been destroyed. In most people's minds the Cathedral was the symbol of Coventry's regeneration, but the Council wanted more than a symbol. They wanted the city centre to be the heart of a thriving community, and grouped around the Cathedral there would be a theatre, art gallery, library, technical college and swimming pool. All these buildings would be new, and the Council felt they should be well designed and purpose built. Naturally the feeling was that 'to be complete, the city should have a University'.

So the City saw the University as an essential element in the town. Links would be built both ways. The University could contribute greatly to Coventry's cultural spectrum, with people meeting through shared facilities, and provide a more universal outlook to local problems. Coventry would provide the environment and physical necessities, and would confront academics with some of the more basic facts of life. There was a strong feeling in the early days that the University should be a technical institution. This is, of course, understandable in view of Coventry's strong industrial tradition, but it would have been surprising if the labour movement, which was the prime mover of the idea, had seen the University as an institution dominated by managerial style.

In 1954 the first practical steps were taken towards setting up a University in Coventry. At the instigation of the Lord Mayor an *ad hoc* committee, called the Council for the Establishment of a University in Coventry, was formed. Chaired by Mr W. H. Stokes, who had been for many years a permanent official of the Amalgamated Engineering Union, it differed from the later, more successful groups in that, although the trade unions did not then (or later) take much active interest in the proposed University, they *were* represented. Later on they were completely ignored.

The Council focused its attention on the notion of a Technical University which would serve the industry of the area. Various MPs were approached; Richard Crossman, in particular, gave his support and, in a letter to Stokes in April 1954, suggested that the University should be modelled on the Massachusetts Institute of Technology. There was considerable opposition in the city from those who believed that expansion of the Technical College would serve just as well, and the two city newspapers took up opposing positions. Others, such as Walter Chinn, the City Education Officer, would not support a University which was an entirely technical institution.

The campaign met with no success. After two years the Council presented its report, reluctantly concluding that 'the establishment of a University of Coventry is not a possibility of the immediate future'. They suggested: 'That this council should remain in being for a further period ... having strong ties with industry, trade unions and bodies representing the general life of the City', but in fact they did not meet again, though various individuals – such as Dr Henry Rees, a lecturer at the Technical College – continued to work for a local university.

On 28 February 1958 the Chancellor of the Exchequer announced to the House of Commons that the government had decided to spend £60 million over the next four years for new university building, involving both expansion of existing universities and the establishment of new universities. This brought new hope to those who wanted a University in Coventry. Dr Henry Rees persuaded the City Architect and a colleage to prepare a plan and a model for a university building, and in December the City Council decided to press for a University in Coventry. It was at this meeting that the two-hundred-acre site now occupied by the University – valuable agricultural and building land worth more than £250,000 at that time, and a great deal more at current values – was earmarked and the proceeds of a penny rate promised.

The Town Clerk, Charles Barratt, and the Education Officer, Walter Chinn, went to see the Chairman of the University Grants Committee for informal talks. They were told that the UGC would be interested, if more public support for the project could be gathered. Specifically they would require that more than one local authority should become involved, and that a considerable amount of money should be promised by local industry.

The next step was to contact Warwickshire County Council. The two education committees met informally and the County gave the idea a rather frosty reception. There was already one University (Birmingham) in Warwickshire, they said, and they could not see what the County had to gain if the University was in Coventry.

The Lord Mayor then issued a formal invitation to Warwickshire County Council to meet the City Council and others interested, with a view to setting up a Promotion Committee. Early in 1960 they met in the Lord Mayor's parlour, in two groups, because of difficulty in arranging a convenient time at short notice. At the first meeting the Warwickshire Education Officer was putting the same discouraging point of view until Sir Robert Aitken, the Vice-Chancellor of Birmingham University, stepped in. He said how very much he welcomed the idea of a new University in Warwickshire and that Birmingham University would give every support. The Bishop of Coventry finally won over the County when he said, 'Let's call it the University of Warwick.' The City at once made this concession over the name and the County promised to meet the City's endowment and provide an equal area of land adjoining that pledged by the City.

Following these meetings the Lord Mayor invited a small group of fourteen friends who had been campaigning for the University to form the nucleus of a Promotion Committee. On 17 March 1960 a letter was sent out in the name of this group to a number of prominent people in Coventry and Warwickshire, inviting them to join the Promotion Committee. The letter was sent to representatives of all sections of the community, except the trade unions. As a result the Executive Committee of the Promotion Committee, which made the application to the UGC, contained no trade unionists, while a third were industrialists. This was significant later, since six of these industrialists were co-opted on to the Council of the University when it was formed in 1965, and they remain there still. Various trade unionists were approached privately by Dr Rees and gave their support, but they seem to have made no attempt to become involved in the Promotion Committee. The trade unions are represented on the governing body of the Lanchester Polytechnic in Coventry, and they appear to have been more concerned with safeguarding the position of the Lanchester with regard to the University than with the University itself.

The Chairman and Deputy Chairman of the Promotion Committee were Lord Rootes and Sir Arnold Hall. Lord Rootes, a local boy made good, seemed the obvious choice to everyone. He was a man very much associated with Coventry, especially because of his work in the War Emergency Committee. The UGC had made it clear that money for the University would be required from other sources, and Lord Rootes was in a position not only to give money himself but also to raise it through his many contacts in industry and his close connexions with the government. Sir Arnold Hall, the Managing Director of Bristol Siddeley, had been involved from fairly early on through his ties with the Lanchester; he has been the Chairman of the University Council since its inception.

The Promotion Committee prepared and submitted an

application to the UGC. A year later, in May 1961, Selwyn Lloyd announced in a written reply in the House of Commons:

The UGC have advised me that, within the scope of the building programme which I have already announced, four new universities, in addition to those which are already being established at Brighton, Norwich and York, should be established as the best means of providing places for some of the increasing number of students who will be coming forward in the coming years. The Committee have advised that three of the four should be at Canterbury, Colchester and Coventry.

The UGC set up an Academic Planning Board for the University; chaired by E. T. Williams, an Oxford don, and currently Warden of Rhodes House, Oxford, it consisted of academics from various universities, except for Sir Arnold Hall, who moved over from the Promotion Committee, and two other businessmen involved in university administration. Until 1965, when the University Charter came into effect, this board controlled the academic affairs and the Promotion Committee the financial business of the University.

Part of the terms of reference of the Academic Planning Board was to appoint the Vice-Chancellor, in consultation with the Promotion Committee and the UGC. On 25 October 1962, over a year after the board first met, Lord Rootes reported to the Promotion Committee that the Board were 'in a position to make progress with the nomination of the first Vice-Chancellor', and they wished to consult the committee on their proposal. The Board's nominee, J. B. Butterworth, Bursar of New College, was presented to the committee at a luncheon four days later. His reputation at Oxford was, perhaps, less that of a distinguished academic, than that of a successful academic entrepreneur, with good connexions in the Stock Exchange and the world of business, who had successfully increased his college's revenue by re-investing some of its capital holdings. The usual procedures went through smoothly and Butterworth's appointment was announced to the Press a fortnight later. After this long delay, some of the local people on the Promotion Committee felt rather resentful that the committee had been given only one choice.

The Vice-Chancellor's appointment was announced at the same time as plans for a full Graduate School of Business Management, 'the first in Britain', and he was pleased to give it his blessing. For a lawyer, teacher and administrator, Butterworth proved to be remarkably attentive to British industry's view of higher education. Addressing the Old Coventrians' Club a year after his appointment, he suggested 'some kind of joint council' where the University would receive 'the criticism, help and advice of industry and commerce' (*Coventry Evening Telegraph*, 9 December 1963). The Vice-Chancellor reiterated his hopes for 'particularly close association' with business in the following month, when Lord Rootes was made Chancellor, and Sir Arnold Hall Pro-Chancellor. It was now clear that 'some kind of joint council' was to be built into the University itself, and that industry was to be represented by large corporate capital. On 21 January 1964 the *Coventry Evening Telegraph* titled its story 'Industrialists to Head University of Warwick'.

The collaboration of men like Rootes and Hall had already brought more tangible benefits than the mere wisdom of the boardroom. Launching the University appeal for £4 million from the Institute of Directors building in Belgrave Square, Rootes announced that he already had £1,150,000 through personal contacts: 'What is more I have a few more friends left' (*Coventry Evening Telegraph*, 9 April 1964). The UGC had insisted on strong local support for a University in Coventry, but the enthusiasm at the Institute presumably justified launching the appeal there rather than in Warwickshire. Six months later some of that enthusiasm led the Institute of Directors to establish a professorship of Business Administration, with the understanding that they would be represented on the appointment board.

Meanwhile other interests had responded to the University's self-declared role of partner with industry. Unilever's grant (given to all the new universities) in 1961 was followed by Courtauld's £75,000. The Registrar acknowledged it with the hope that the research to be done 'would be of particular interest to the firm' (*Coventry Evening Telegraph*, 17 February 1964). Pressed Steel Fisher earmarked their gift for a Chair of

Industrial Relations. A grant of £40,000 from the Volkswagen Foundation, ICI Fellowships and Dunlop Scholarships followed. Butterworth suggested in his first Annual Report that 'No one would wish a University founded in Warwickshire to develop into something like a liberal arts college'. If such a danger had ever existed, surely it was long past?

In that report of 1965 the Vice-Chancellor also referred to the 'local ethos' which favoured a school strong in science and engineering. Part of that ethos centred on the Lanchester, a highly respected college of technology in Coventry, which some City Councillors had believed would become a university in its own right. In the early stages of planning the University, the Lanchester's governors had expressed their interest in a fusion of the two schools, and finally in 1964 the University Promotion Committee replied favourably. The City Education Committee entered negotiations, the substance of which it did not discuss in public. In private, the University set terms: complete absorption of the College, and acceptance of only those Lanchester staff and students that it wished to take. The opinion of the College governors was that there should be no vetting of staff or students, and democratic representation on governing bodies of the University. A sub-committee met with Butterworth and two other representatives, and by March 1965 a fairly detailed plan of union was announced. It was approved by the City, although fears were expressed that the UGC and the Minister might have doubts.

In August the fears were realized: the Department of Education and Science rejected the plans as being likely to prejudice lower-level studies, and tie up too much of the limited money available for universities. But the Minister's letter came before the City delegation had put their case to him: there was 'surprise and anger' in Coventry. Nothing came of an appeal to the Department by the City, as the Chairman of the Education Committee, Councillor Locksley, predicted. Time had been of the essence, he explained, and although the City's representation had been before the UGC by April, they had discovered in June that the Vice-Chancellor of the University had not yet presented the University's submission: 'So we lost two valuable months. I was aggrieved about this because I felt that apart from the urgency we should have been doing this together' (*Coventry Evening Telegraph*, 23 September 1965). Other councillors were unwilling to blame the University, but without doubt many citizens of Coventry had questions in their minds. After many attempts and disappointments, they had brought a University to Coventry. And now they wondered what influence they were going to have in its development.

Development was going on at a great pace. Or was it? Many months of tact and enthusiasm had gone into cultivating the British corporate élite, but buildings and governing structure were dealt with in a rather more hurried fashion. Because of the year's delay in appointing a Vice-Chancellor, and further delays in establishing a University planning office, as late as the winter of 1963 there were virtually no plans in progress. Even the location of the site was not finally decided. Yet eight professors had been promised accommodation within nine months, and the first students were due to arrive a year after that; consultation, planning and construction of permanent university buildings usually takes five years or so. The solution was a small, completely self-contained block of buildings to serve as interim accommodation for the University while plans could be drawn up for the main site. At this time the best guess was that the publication of the Robbins Report would result in massive, immediate expansion, and the main site was planned with this in mind. Only at the end of 1963 was it decided that the 1966 bulge of students would be absorbed largely by the older universities. Credit squeezes and cuts in grants played havoc with the plans. Warwick is left with a sprawling, fragmented campus, a fitting expression of the lack of early planning.

A consistent feature in this planning was the insistence of the Vice-Chancellor that all plans should be geared to his megalithic notions of a University of twenty thousand or even twenty-five thousand students. Hence, even in its initial stages, plans had to be in line with setting down a megalithic infrastructure. The large area was set out with a divider and a ruler: Administration nearly one mile from the library and teaching buildings, student residences and social building segregated again, like the service stations on a detour from the motorway.

Short-term, interim amenities were discouraged in the name of the plan, and the first generations of students were to be sacrificed in the cause of expansion and high rate of growth. But no documentary evidence has ever been adduced to show that this growth-rate and this twenty-thousand target had ever been given government or UGC approval, or that they ever existed as anything more than an ambition of the Vice-Chancellor and of his close Council advisers.

Much as the development plan should have determined the physical structure of the University, the statutes were intended to define the powers and responsibilities of all its members. Their adoption was also a rushed affair, but with less excuse. The first knowledge Warwick academic staff in general had of the statutes was from the draft posted to them three days before they were asked to give their approval. They did so, perhaps without sufficiently reflecting on the possible implications of section 5 (5), giving the Vice-Chancellor power to exclude any student without explanation or right of appeal, or the dangers in a co-opting clause (15 (1) (D)), which could enable a powerful and united group of men, once appointed, to perpetuate their power indefinitely and hence mould the University (see p. 28). But two days is a short time to consider a constitution, and in any case the way in which the statutes were used was to prove almost more important than their content.

Equally important was the membership of the Council that took power in March 1965. The Promotion Committee and Academic Planning Board disappeared, but many of their most important figures did not. The new Lord Rootes, Sir Arnold Hall, Gilbert Hunt, Lord Iliffe, Sir Stanley Harley, Sir William Lyons and R. J. Kerr-Muir all became members of Council. It is important to note not only who *did* transfer from the Promotion Committee to the Council, but who did *not*. Some of the original Committee were politely given places on the University's Court – an almost powerless body which meets only once a year. The only layman who was not an industrialist who moved on to Council was the Bishop of Coventry: among those who were not co-opted to Council were Sister A. G. Grace, Dr G. S. Atkinson (Principal of Rugby Technical College), Miss J. D. Browne (Principal of the City of Coventry College of Education), the Congregationalist Minister the Rev. D. H. Dale, the Catholic Canon R. Walsh, Dr H. Rees (one of the most active of the original promoters), Mr H. Walker (the Headmaster of King Henry the Eighth School), and a number of civic officials, aldermen and others. These people may all have been too busy and too much committed to other duties to serve on Council, nor were they necessarily the best people to represent the local community on that body; but the self-perpetuating character of an oligarchy of industrialists was at this stage brought several steps closer. There were also six *ex officio* members of local authorities and six (now eight) members of Senate. But the evolution of the University was to be most affected by the ethos of the very powerful men from industry; men who were prepared to work closely with a Vice-Chancellor who was willing to work closely with them. And the ultimate effect came to be the creation, not of a democratic academic community, but a 'well-managed operation', assisting the business corporation and emulating some of its more dubious methods.

Nor did the University show much interest in working with the City which had done so much to bring it into being. Relations were, in fact, often strained. Hostility was first aroused in the city over an alleged deal done over the heads of the City Council which threatened to destroy the beauty of the main road past the University (see p. 143).

Later on the University snubbed the City Council over proposals to share sports and library facilities. The City were thinking of building a large sports stadium and centre near the University to serve all the educational institutions in the city as well as other independent athletic groups. The University, in the person of Pro-Vice-Chancellor Harrison, told the Council that it had not got any money for such projects. On being offered a share in return for the land to build the centre on (land originally a gift from the City), the University said that, only if an equivalent proportion of new land was given, could they release land for such a project. Meanwhile the University was planning a sports centre of its own. At the present time the University is planning to spend a large sum on a swimming pool, whilst Coventry has one of the finest in the country.

As we have seen, Coventry City Council was crucial in preparing and bringing the case for a University in Coventry to the UGC in 1959. Their initiative was in keeping with the whole concept of city planning and organization which the Labour Party had used during its thirty years' control of the council. It is ironic that their ideal of community involvement and democratic government should have been ignored in what was, during this period, their favoured child.

It is appropriate to end with the words of Alderman G. E. Hodgkinson, Lord Mayor of Coventry in 1944–5, one of the chief architects of the rebuilding and replanning of Coventry when the City emerged from the ruins of the war, and a member of the University Court:

The members of a Labour-controlled City Council who applied their enthusiasms for the 'University Idea' gave it practical and moral support in the formation days. Amongst other things, it wanted a University of original design in accordance with native thrustfulness, a physical academic link between the Lanchester Polytechnic, a close association between 'town and gown', open-door facilities in library services and playing fields, and coordinated shopping and banking arrangements on the campus to avoid unnecessary conflict in planning effective liaison in these matters. The town and gown concept appears to have been overlaid, swamped or forgotten by the dominating business interests. Those who pay the piper least are playing most of the tune. Industry, banking and commerce are at the 'commanding heights' of the University, doing their utmost to keep town and gown apart. Student, academic, democratic and community interests are relegated to the level of second-class citizenship (unpublished letter to the *Guardian*, part published in the *Morning Star*, 2 March 1970).

The Power of the Council

It has been shown that the Vice-Chancellor, soon after his appointment, proposed 'some kind of joint council' between industry and the University (p. 23). In the event such a joint council proved to be unnecessary, since it was provided by the direct

representation of industrialists on the University's governing
Council itself. The presence of a majority of lay members upon
a university's Council is not, of course, unusual. What is unusual is the mode of their appointment, under section 15 (1)
(D) of the statutes of the University of Warwick:

Such other persons, not being members of the academic staff or
salaried officers of the University, and not exceeding ten in all, as
may be co-opted by the Council.

In older provincial universities at least a proportion of the lay
members of Council are appointed by the University's Court –
a very large, inactive body, representative of a wide spread of
civic interests and organizations. For example the University
of Birmingham, which is not notorious for its advanced democratic constitution, has no co-opted members on its Council:
its lay membership is made up of the Lord Mayor of Birmingham, five persons appointed by the City Council, and sixteen
members appointed by the Court.

But at Warwick the majority of lay members, if they acted
together, could be virtually self-perpetuating. The two most
powerful officers – the Pro-Chancellor (Sir Arnold Hall) and
the Treasurer (R. J. Kerr-Muir) – remain on Council so long as
they continue to hold office. The 'co-opted' members serve for
a three-year term (section 15 (2) (F)), but may then, if they
wish, be 'co-opted' for further terms. Where new members are
co-opted (as Messrs Mead, Tuke and Young have been), it is
generally understood that their names 'emerge' after consultation between the Vice-Chancellor and the Pro-Chancellor.
Since the term of service of local authority nominees may be
limited to three years (all the Labour members were dropped
after the Conservatives won control of Coventry City Council),
the 'co-opted' members are likely to be entrenched in the Council's most powerful committees; and indeed we find two recently 'co-opted' members – Tuke and Mead – together with
Kerr-Muir and Butterworth, controlling the crucial seven-man
Finance and General Purposes Committee. While all co-opted
members are not regular attenders at Council, they have been
present in force at crucial meetings where contested issues have
arisen and even a few of them, acting together with the Vice-

Chancellor and officers and one or two academics, can be expected to dominate decisions.*

'Industry' has therefore been able to influence the University, at the level of its planning, financing and development, at a relatively-low cost in terms of promotion and donations. Some of the aims of a 'private university' have been achieved within the shell of public money and public legitimation. It is true that the University's Foundation Fund Appeal met with a generous response, exceeding £2½ million, in the main in substantial covenants from industry. It is possible, however, to exaggerate the extent of open-handed charity which was involved on the part of some of the benefactors. The Foundation Fund Appeal brochure noted that:

In terms of the Income Tax Act 1952, gifts of money for research related to, or for technical education of a kind specially requisite for persons employed in, the business of the donor (or for research related to the class of trade to which the business of the donor belongs) may be treated as an expense of the business for Income Tax and Profits Tax purposes. . . . Further details may be obtained from the Vice-Chancellor.

(This meant that, with tax at 7s 9d in the £, a gift of £100,000 could be met, under a ten-year covenant, at £6,125 p.a.; a gift of £5,000 at £306 p.a.)

It is not therefore surprising that when Ralph Harris, Director of the Institute of Economic Affairs Ltd, wrote to Jack Butterworth (4 December 1968) soliciting his support for the movement headed by Professor Max Beloff, Sir Sydney Caine, Professor H. S. Ferns and others for an 'independent university', he should express his support:

I have always been attracted by the idea of an independent university and believe that if properly organized it might acquire the considerable funds needed from industry and private support. As a Vice-Chancellor of a state university, I think it might be better if I were not to sign your document. On the other hand, I wanted to let you know of my interest in your proposal.

* It is not suggested that all the co-opted members necessarily act together as a bloc with the Pro-Chancellor and Vice-Chancellor.

'Academic excellence', the letter continued, may best be preserved 'in an institution which is totally independent.'

We will examine later how far business interests may have actually influenced academic excellence or general policy at Warwick. The point to note here is that this kind of 'independence' is a mirage. The independence desired is from the State (and its democratic or bureaucratic controls) on the one hand, from the pressures of staff and of students on the other. This independence would only be the other side of the coin of a subordinate dependence upon 'industry'.

The World of Industry

On the Council of the University of Warwick we find the following:

Pro-Chancellor   Sir Arnold Hall
Chairman and Managing Director, Hawker Siddeley Group Ltd
Director, Phoenix Assurance Co. Ltd
Director, Lloyds Bank Ltd *

Treasurer   R. J. Kerr-Muir
Director, Courtaulds Ltd

Council Members   Gilbert Hunt
Managing Director, Rootes Motors Ltd
Director, Reed Paper Group

A. F. Tuke
Director, Barclays Bank Ltd
Vice-Chairman, Barclays D.C.O.

Sir Richard Young
Chairman, Alfred Herbert Ltd
Director, Rugby Portland Cement Ltd

Lord Rootes
Chairman, Rootes Motors Ltd

* At least thirteen of the thirty-one directors of Lloyds Bank are governors, pro-chancellors, etc. of universities and colleges; the thirteen hold seventeen such posts.

Sir William Lyons
Chairman, Jaguar Cars Ltd
Deputy Chairman, British Leyland Motor
Holdings Ltd

Lord Iliffe
Chairman, Coventry Newspapers Ltd
Vice-Chairman, Birmingham Post and Mail Ltd

Sir Stanley Harley
Chairman, Coventry Gauge and Tool Ltd
Director of fifteen other companies
President, Coventry Conservative Association

J. R. Mead
Accountant: director of forty-two small companies

The Right Reverend the Bishop of Coventry

It is this concentration of business interests at the top of the power structure at Warwick which is unusual, rather than the involvement of industry in financing scientific and economic research. A closer look at some of the key figures involved on Council sheds considerable light on the world of industry and the nature of Warwick's involvement in it.

Sir Arnold Hall

Sir Arnold Hall is an engineer of exceptional brilliance. Born in 1915, he obtained a First with distinction in engineering at Cambridge. After doing research there and at the Royal Aircraft Establishment, Farnborough, including work with Sir Frank Whittle on the first jet engine, he became a Professor at Imperial College at the age of thirty. Six years later he was made head of the Royal Aircraft Establishment, where he headed the investigation into the Comet crashes. At thirty-nine he was knighted; the following year, 1955, he joined the Hawker Siddeley Group as a director. His career there culminated in his appointment as Managing Director in 1963, to which the chairmanship was added in 1967. He has sat on innumerable governmental and semi-governmental committees on the aerospace industry, is a member of the Athenaeum, and a Fellow of the Royal Society.

But over this distinguished career, in which Sir Arnold has moved easily between government, industry and academic life, there hangs one question mark. His entry in *Who's Who*, while describing in great detail the rest of his career, omits the fact that from 1958 to 1963 he was Vice-Chairman and Managing Director of Bristol Siddeley Engines Ltd.

On 22 March 1967 the Minister of Technology announced in the House of Commons that Bristol Siddeley 'had repaid to the Ministry a sum of £3,960,000, and that the effect of the repayment had been to reduce the profits made by the firm on sales at fixed prices totalling approximately £16½ million' (*Second Special Report of the Committee of Public Accounts* (hereafter CPA/2), HC 571 1966–7, para. 1). An inquiry (the Wilson Committee) was set up to investigate the whole matter, and in addition the Committee of Public Accounts made an independent investigation of the narrower question of the negotiation of the original contracts, which involved engine overhauls carried out by Bristol Siddeley for the government.

Following these two inquiries a third was set up, by the Committee of Public Accounts, to look into certain apparent discrepancies between the evidence given by the company's representatives to the CPA and the findings of the broader inquiry by the Wilson Committee.

To quote this third inquiry:

The evidence paints a picture of negligence and irresponsibility in the conduct of the Company's financial administration which your committee found hard to credit in a Company of this standing, even after making the utmost allowances for the many and great difficulties the Company was facing at a critical juncture in its affairs. This applies particularly to the important role played by Mr Davidson, as the Director responsible for the Company's contracts with the Ministry, and to the manner in which the Executive Committee exercised its collective responsibility for financial administration (*Third Special Report of the Committee for Public Accounts* (hereafter CPA/3), HC 192 1967–8, para. 21).

That the profits realized on these contracts were exorbitant was agreed by all concerned. Typical figures for selected engines in 1959–60 and 1960–61 were:

	% profit on cost	
	1959–60	1960–61
Olympus	51·8	80·3
Viper	44·8	135·2
Sapphire 7	50·7	124·9

(*Wilson Committee Report*, HC 129 1967–8, paras. 80–81.)

The Wilson Committee found that these rates of profit 'were being achieved as a result of false and misleading representations on the part of the Company's estimating and negotiating committee' (para. 83).

The crucial point at issue throughout the two CPA inquiries was whether this state of affairs was known to the Board of Directors. Mr Davidson and Sir Reginald Verdon-Smith (Chairman of BSE at the time) insisted that the Board was not aware of this. Yet it emerges from the Wilson Committee's report that the Executive Committee of the company was well aware of the facts, having considered two reports on the engine overhauls contract, one in June and September 1960, and the other in September 1961.

The Chairman of the Executive Committee at the time was the Managing Director of Bristol Siddeley, Sir Arnold Hall. An Executive Committee minute of June 1960 read:

Engine Repair Financial Report: Sir Arnold Hall has written to Mr Davidson on a number of minor points which were currently being looked into. It was noted that Orenda profitability was low and that this stemmed from the close surveillance on this contract exercised by the customer from London [in fact a Canadian Government contract]. It was noted also that Viper overhauls were less profitable than might have been expected . . . (quoted in CPA/3, para. 184).

At that time Viper overhauls were running at a profit rate of 44·8 per cent.

Despite the fact that the crucial point at issue was whether the Board had knowledge of what was going on at the time, Sir Arnold Hall was never called to submit evidence to either of the inquiries conducted by the Committee of Public Accounts. When Verdon-Smith suggested

... it may be your wish, if you want to explore this point in depth, that you should, perhaps, ask the Managing Director of Bristol Siddeley at that time to answer this question (CPA/2, para. 428),

he was rebuked by the Committee's chairman.

As the Wilson Committee report put it:

The facts to which we have referred leave no room for doubt that the Executive Directors of BSE planned in their budgets, from the earliest years of the Company's existence, to obtain huge profits from the Department's overhauls; that they were soon made aware that the achievements were even better than those which they had sought; and that they approved of the trend of events (para. 82).

One further point on Sir Arnold Hall. Three documents were found among the Vice-Chancellor's files which were put out by the Economic League. Two were sent to the Vice-Chancellor by Hall. The League is an employers' organization with two main aims: first, to foster the 'free enterprise spirit' by propaganda, verbal and written (twenty-two million leaflets in 1968); secondly, to oppose 'all subversive forces – in whatever their origin and inspiration – that seek to undermine the security of Britain in general and British industry in particular'. In 1968 the League spent £266,000 on such activities. One hundred and fifty-four firms, including British Leyland, Guest Keen & Nettlefold, Tate & Lyle and Barclays Bank, gave donations totalling £61,000.

Two of the documents sent to Butterworth were issues of the League's *Two-Minute News Review* on the activities of the Radical Student Alliance and the Revolutionary Socialist Student Federation. The other, headed 'Confidential', was part of a survey by 'a team of expert investigators' conducted on behalf of the League on 'the growth of extreme left-wing activity among students'. It consists in the main of case-studies: the general impression is that rank-and-file revolutionary students tend to come from broken homes, have personality problems, are dirty and unkempt, take drugs, suffer from acne, are easily

'led', etc. The investigators do, however, allow that some become revolutionaries because of 'a genuine belief that the university "system" is archaic, inflexible, repressive and out of
date', and many of their conclusions are considered in
tone.

As for Sir Arnold Hall's company, Hawker Siddeley, it was
in 1969 the eighteenth largest in the country in terms of assets
(£250 million) and fifth largest in terms of employment
(98,000). It is heavily involved in defence work.

Gilbert Hunt and Rootes

The Rootes family has, of course, been associated with the
University from its very beginning. Gilbert Hunt, who became
Managing Director of Rootes in 1967, first got to know Lord
Rootes through involvement in the University Foundation
Committee's activities. He is of interest here largely as an
example of the style of the modern manager, and managerial-
ism is a major product of Warwick's involvement with industry
(see sections from the Tyzack Report, pp. 136–43).

Gilbert Hunt was born in 1915. Educated at Malvern College, he then joined the Hawker Siddeley Group, working his
way up until he became Director and General Manager of their
subsidiary, High Duty Alloys. In 1960 he was appointed
Managing Director of Massey-Ferguson (UK) Ltd; finally in
1967 he became Managing Director of Rootes, soon after
Chrysler acquired a major interest in the company. At the time
Rootes was having its worst year ever: it reported a loss of
nearly £11 million. The appointment of Gilbert Hunt to replace the second Lord Rootes, along with massive injections of
funds from Chrysler and the British government, was intended
to bring about the necessary spectacular recovery. In 1968
Rootes made £1·4 million profits, but in 1969 they were back
in the red again. It is clear that unless the Avenger is a huge
success, the company will be once more on the brink of
disaster.

But what of Gilbert Hunt? Newspaper cuttings throw some
interesting light on the sort of man he is:

A soft-spoken, grey-haired fifty-two-year-old, Hunt is a firm
disciple of North American business methods. . . . Apart from the

Rolls-Royce Phantom V, Buick and Triumph 2000 he keeps in his stable, Hunt knows little about cars. But when it comes to questions of productivity and business methods, he is in his element (*Financial Times* Diary, 22 March 1967).

'When you take over a job like this you have to be tough immediately. It's no good waiting five years to be tough – you'll never do it. The hatchet gets blunt. . . . People in British industry are not numerate enough. It is not sufficient to have a good idea. It must be quantified to make absolutely certain that it is viable. Everything must be worked out in mathematical terms' (*Sunday Times* Business News, 1 October 1967).

'I rebuilt Rootes around an eight-man élite. . . . This is in effect the policy-making instrument of the company, and answerable only to the Board.' Hunt has also instilled a new pride and confidence in Rootes employees. 'There are no secrets between the top management – my key people. I involve them because I believe it is the vitality, the brain power and the judgement of these key men working with me which is going to make or break the company' (*Daily Express*, 4 March 1968).

It is hardly surprising that such a man should be an enthusiastic supporter of greater 'efficiency' in the University, as proposed by the Tyzack Report. Nor is it surprising that Mr Hunt once spoke heatedly, in Council, against students who had been demonstrating outside a Rootes factory, and asked if they could be disciplined and their local education authority be notified. He also suggested that he might find difficulty in defending Rootes' contribution to the University against adverse comments by his fellow directors. (It is proper to add that the Chairman of Council, Sir Arnold Hall, firmly resisted the implications of both suggestions.)

Rootes gave £2,000 to the Industrial Trust last year. This organization is much more secretive than the Economic League, but similar in purpose. In an article in the *Observer* (19 October 1969) Paul Ferris described how he had phoned several firms who had donated money to the Industrial Trust in order to find out what the Trust did. No one would tell him. Then Lord Chandos (of Associated Electrical Industries, and a member of Warwick's Promotion Committee) phoned Mr Ferris and told him that its work was 'non-political, and in the field of industrial harmony'. When Ferris wondered whether they ·kept an eye on 'troublemakers', and said he was not really clear about their activities, Lord Chandos replied, 'You're not meant to be clear.'

A. F. Tuke and Barclays Bank

As the Vice-Chancellor's files say:

I regard the association between Barclays Bank and the University of Warwick as especially close. Not only are we Bankers to the University and the only Bank represented on the site, but we have endowed a Chair, the Chairman of our Local Board serves on the Finance Committee, and our Chairman and the Vice-Chancellor are friends of long standing who, during their time, have been jointly involved in the problems of University finance, i.e. the University of Oxford. I cannot think, therefore, that any university could have a claim on the Bank's favourable consideration of a need stronger than that of the University of Warwick.

The 'Chairman of our Local Board' is Mr A. F. Tuke, member of Council at Warwick. The Vice-Chancellor used to be Bursar of New College, Oxford, and member of the Hebdomadal Council. And the 'Chair' with which Barclays endowed the University? This was the Chair in Management Information Systems in the Centre of Industrial and Business Studies. The *Coventry Evening Telegraph* of 12 October 1967 reported:

Mr W. G. Bryan, a Vice-Chairman of Barclays Bank, said:
'We are very enthusiastic about this joint venture, which we feel will be to our mutual advantage, and will also benefit banking and the business world generally....
'At present, most of the research in the area of management information services is being carried out in the United States. Now similar facilities will be available in Britain, and we look forward to the opportunity of keeping in close touch with the professor appointed to the chair.' The creation of the new chair is warmly welcomed by the University's Vice-Chancellor, Mr J. B. Butterworth, who said it would strengthen still further the close association with industry and commerce....
'The particular points we would like to see developed are all focused on the problem of putting a value as far as possible on the

information provided, on the selection of priorities in the presentation of information to management, the methods of presentation, the economics of computerizing the information processes, and so on.

'Efficiently conducted research in this field, allied to the work on operational research, would be of importance nationally, both in encouraging the use of computers where firms are slow to recognize their value, and in discouraging uneconomic use of computers in those firms where computers are in fashion.'

It will be the sixth chair to be created at the University in the field of social studies as a result of support from industry, commerce, trusts and foundations.

The University's close relation with industry and commerce 'spring from the conviction that a new university has a unique opportunity to experiment and in the case of Warwick to make a significant contribution in the field of industrial and business studies'.

The University emphasizes that it is also aware of the fact that the abler undergraduates have often shown a reluctance to enter commerce and industry.

'It is incumbent upon universities, therefore, as the prime producers of high-level manpower over the whole range of industrial development, to develop courses and subjects which will equip its graduates for problems they will subsequently face in industry and commerce', it is stated.

Barclays' concern for benefiting 'the business world generally' is also evident from their £4,750 donation to the Economic League last year.

Mr A. F. Tuke, in addition to being a Director of Barclays Bank, is also Vice-Chairman of Barclays D.C.O. This bank is a considerable force in the finance world of southern Africa. Two other businesses with interests in southern Africa are represented on the Council. British Leyland, whose Vice-Chairman, Sir William Lyons, is on the Council at Warwick, has been rapidly expanding its manufacturing facilities in South Africa, and Hawker Siddeley have recently formed a South African subsidiary.

One prime social function of a university is to inquire freely and to criticize freely. And the more managed, the more planned, the more 'efficient' the rest of society grows, the more important this function becomes. In pursuing this task in as sensitive an area as Africa, some staff and students might prefer their university not to embrace too closely industries and businesses that have large stakes in the racialist police state of South Africa.

One of the pervasive myths of the mid-twentieth century is that with the replacement of the old-style entrepreneur and tycoon by the propertyless manager, there has come about a qualitative change to 'managerial' capitalism. The new manager is seen as running the system 'in the national interest' rather than in the interests of the propertied class. Professor Carl Kaysen, a distinguished American economist, has gone so far as to describe the giant corporation as 'soulful'. The economic and political system as a whole is described as 'pluralist', that is, one in which different interest groups form around different issues, with no clear-cut social divisions.

Where does the University fit into this picture? Professor Clark Kerr, who ran the Berkeley campus of the University of California where many have located the origins of the student movement, answered this question in his book *The Uses of the University*. The University provides skilled manpower and facilities for basic research. And it produces the culture and ideology of the pluralist system.

Thus, Warwick as the Massachusetts Institute of Technology of the Midlands, and Butterworth as a latter-day Clark Kerr.

But the world of industry is emphatically *not* a world of a neutral technocracy working for the benefit of all. It is a world indifferent to the equities of government contracting, a world where excess profits can be milked from the ordinary people, a world of efficiency and quantification in the interests of profit, of connivance at racialist exploitation in southern Africa, of spying on workers and teachers.

In this alternative view, what is our picture of the economic system, and of the way the University fits into it?

In modern capitalism most important industries, and especially those predominant in the Midlands, are dominated by a handful of giant firms. Despite this, it is a competitive world; the competition is not of the static type found in outdated economics textbooks, but dynamic; for, above all, capitalism is an economic system with an inbuilt drive for growth, for accumulation. In an economy based on private property, growth means the accumulation of privately owned assets. This process requires profits, just as it always has done. And the drive for profits in a world dominated by a small number of firms is above all a drive for control.

It is only natural that this drive for control should extend to the University. There is no area in life which is not penetrated by the needs of the giant firm. The University offers skilled manpower and research facilities. It also offers them largely at the expense of the general public: Warwick has had six times as much government money as private. The extension of corporate power over the University need not yield an immediate return for the investment of time and money; the modern giant firm takes a long-term view of its activities.

Chapter 2
The Student Response

Student Life at Warwick

The first undergraduates came to Warwick in 1965. There were about 450 students working in just one set of buildings, the East Site. There were close links between staff and students, and the pioneering spirit also made for unity. Various activities were under way soon after the start of term: sports teams were organized, a magazine was founded, and within a couple of weeks a duplicated newspaper was produced. In this first year everybody lived off campus in digs, so that to be on site meant being around the library or the common room if no lectures were being given. The compactness of the East Site meant that a student could hardly avoid being involved in whatever was going on. When Warwick first started there was a feeling that you were needed, that things wouldn't happen unless you made them.

As a new university Warwick had no traditions to guide it, and in fact it was this potential freedom to experiment and change existing academic practices which attracted many of the staff. Those students who were interested in their subjects generally seemed quite satisfied with the quality of the teaching and the content of the courses. Criticism of teaching and course content varies, of course, between departments, but there has never been any large movement of complaint about teaching. However, students who have wanted to change subjects have not always found it easy to do so, and methods of assessment have been a controversial issue: many departments, through their staff/student liaison committees, have discussed alternative plans, and many of them now have provision for assessed written work to replace examinations.

Those first students expected student life to become richer as the University grew. Yet the changes did not always live up to these expectations. As the new buildings opened the campus spread out. Coming from the Coventry–Kenilworth road, the first set of buildings is known collectively as the East Site. This now houses the Administration, the appointments office, the bank and various departments. To reach the next set of buildings, which includes the halls of residence and the social building, Rootes Hall, takes a walk of up to ten minutes from the East Site, down a hill, through a wood and up a further rise. To reach the library and the science blocks, known collectively as the Main Site, is a further five-minute walk from Rootes Hall. The University site as a whole is also removed from surrounding communities: it is about three miles from Coventry and two and a half from Kenilworth. The isolation is reflected in the lack of ties between the University and the colleges in Coventry, particularly the Lanchester Polytechnic and the Coventry College of Education.

It is against this physical background that student life at Warwick must be set. Movement within the University is difficult, but circumstances also hinder relations with the outside world. Indeed, 'The Outside World' is a particularly meaningful phrase at Warwick, especially for those who live on the site in halls of residence (at present there are about 800, from a student population of around 1,800). It is quite possible not to move from the campus for weeks: there is food, albeit poor, in the refectory, a shop with grossly inadequate stocks of groceries, entertainments of various sorts, and a bar.

Whether or not one can draw a causal link between this situation and the growth of political activism over the past couple of years is arguable. That there has been such a growth is less doubtful. The start of the University's third year was a significant watershed. Up to that point there had been very little action on campus, and any issues were largely internal Union affairs. The previous spring had seen the first of the big Vietnam demonstrations in London, which a few members of the University had attended. In the week before term started in October the US Ambassador to Britain was due to open the Benefactors' Hall of Residence, a sumptuous block donated by an anonymous benefactor to promote Anglo-American understanding. Enough students (including some American exchange students) were around to stage a small anti-war protest.

Although it was small, it was probably the first demonstration on campus. It was certainly the first to involve the police on campus, and it was the first to involve students from the Lanchester Polytechnic and Canley College of Education.

From this time on the University became more active in a political – though not in a party political – sense. Controversial speakers, such as an official from the South Vietnamese Embassy and Major Patrick Wall, MP, were heckled. All the same, most people regarded Warwick as quite mild as such things were going at the time. Such activism as occurred was usually sporadic, and there was little feeling of a continuing ongoing current. This was reflected in the general easy-going attitude of the majority of students. Events which stirred people up were seemingly little connected and difficult to predict. In December 1968 someone painted an entire Winnie-the-Pooh story on the paved path between Rootes Hall and the library (it was, incidentally, written in such a way that to read it one would have to walk backwards). Soon afterwards workmen appeared to overturn the offending paving stones. Protest meetings were held, petitions were circulated, a rash of slogans appeared around the University designed to proclaim the right to daub on university buildings – some solely about Pooh, and some attempting to widen the political content. One such included a reference to the May 1968 troubles in France, declaring in red paint 'Le Chienlit, c'est J.B.' Work on overturning the paving stones was halted, and half an A. A. Milne story written backwards was left to face the elements. Not a trace remains today, but the effect on the students was of a more permanent nature.

Early the following term, Warwick was the first University to come forward in support of the LSE students in their dispute about (amongst other things) the placing of steel gates inside the LSE buildings. It was decided at a lunchtime meeting (which was not an official Union General Meeting) to stage a twenty-four-hour token sit-in in the library building. Those who had sat-in came to the Union General Meeting in the evening to present their case, and the largest meeting to that date voted in favour of continuing the occupation. Following the sit-in, the students marched into Coventry with the intention of trying to explain to people what the issues were. Whilst this march was in progress departments received requests for names of those people not attending lectures or seminars that morning. These requests had the effect of uniting staff and students against what was considered an unjustifiable intrusion.

Other activity during the year included an attempt to save the job of a workman who was sacked for disobeying what he regarded as pointless orders from his superior. He was popular with the students, and one of the reasons for his popularity was that he did 'unofficial' jobs for students. It was fairly inevitable that he would go, but student pressure took the matter up to an appeal to Council.

Mention has been made of the Students' Union. The Union has been in formal existence since the start of the University's second year. The importance with which students regarded it is indicated by the relatively low polls for Union elections. The Union structure is based on the President, who has a ten-man executive, but constitutionally the sovereign body is the Students' Representative Council (SRC), which is made up of representatives from each academic department. Probably most students regard the Union as a glorified travel agency, a negotiator with the Administration, a distributor of LEA grants to the various clubs and societies, a promoter of poorly attended dances, and little else. Occasionally it might prove useful to carry out the wishes of a general meeting, but the feeling has certainly grown that the UGM is in a position to decide fundamental issues, and the elected Union has to take second place to this. The Union undoubtedly does do useful work some of the time – as in its tenacious handling of the negotiations over the Union Building over several years (see pp. 60–70). In the Union's own terms, however, its most substantial advances since its inception have been the gain of a sabbatical president and, more significantly, increased full-time help with the administration of the Union.

Throughout the development of the University there has been a growing sense of frustration, coupled with a feeling of isolation. There were high hopes on all sides for Warwick when it started. The first year began well, yet the whole thing has apparently turned sour. Students grew to be wary of the use of the University's youth as a reason for the non-appearance of certain important improvements affecting student life. There was, for example, feeling that the University Administration might have its priorities wrong when plans for a chapel were announced before those for a much needed Arts Centre and theatre.

Even the good staff/student relations of the first year appear not to have lasted. The personal tutor system, designed to help in this respect, cannot really function without some basis in good staff/student social relations. Yet Warwick has become a place which staff leave at five o'clock, and also a place which students leave. The weekend exodus was one of the earliest tendencies to establish itself, especially in the second and third years. There would be virtually nothing happening at the weekend around the social building, which would have been the centre for any activity.

In October 1969 there was an easy-going student body, which had nevertheless been known to erupt. Even so, the left-wing element among the students was not particularly strong, and Union politics were not considered of much significance. There was, however, still the unsolved issue of the Union Building.

The Course of the Struggle

A mixture of boredom, dissatisfaction with courses, general frustration and apathy produced a restless mood at Warwick throughout the autumn term of 1969. Union meetings were fairly well attended (150–200), but were generally bad-tempered affairs. There was little political activity apart from the spate of anti-Springbok demonstrations; these provoked much debate about whether the Union should pay any fines incurred, but the debate proved to be academic since no Warwick students were ever fined. Yet the Springbok issue was important, because almost for the first time political discussion was taking place in the Union on an issue not directly related to students.

On 27 January 1970 a meeting was organized by the Union to discuss the long-delayed social buildings. The Vice-Chancellor was invited to attend, but sent instead the Assistant

Vice-Chancellor and the Registrar; both these men were
recent appointments. They were questioned by the students:
'When is the final decision to be taken?' 'How many students
will the new building accommodate?' 'Who takes the final decision?' Frequently the students were given evasive answers,
or the all-too-convenient reply: 'I haven't been here very long,
and I'm afraid I can't answer that question.' The administrators
left after being thanked from the floor for having so successfully hanged themselves in public.

After that meeting the students formulated very simple but
very direct demands to put before the Building Committee of
Council. They wanted a totally integrated staff/student building, jointly controlled by the users, and if this was not possible then an entirely separate building, to be totally student-
controlled.

Four students went along to the Building Committee on
Monday 2 February 1970. They were given a four-page document stating the University's position on the social building.
This document was supposed to have been given to the students
several days earlier, but somehow this had been overlooked.
The student representatives were thus at a great disadvantage,
having had little time to digest information with which the
members of the Building Committee were familiar. The
students handed out copies of the motion passed at the Union
meeting, containing their demands. The chairman, Gilbert
Hunt, began by saying that he was offended by the wording of
the motion, which reminded him of the type of demands put
forward by the unions at Rootes in Coventry. Having scolded
the recalcitrant students and having listened to their demands,
the Committee then asked the students to leave so that they
could come to a decision.

That evening in Rootes Hall two meetings were taking place.
The Union Executive, a body not noted for its militancy, was
drawing up plans for a twenty-four-hour token sit-in in the
Registry, to demonstrate that the students were serious in their
demands. Across the corridor the Socialist Society was also
in discussion; the feeling of this meeting emerged as a 'wait
and see' stance until the Building Committee's position was
known. The socialists were opposed to the idea of a 'twenty-

four-hour tea-party in the Registry', believing that an occupation should be undertaken seriously or not at all. The two meetings came together, and one had the weird spectacle of the Union bureaucracy trying to persuade the Socialist Society to support their plans for direct action. At a Union meeting the following day, attended by about four hundred students, a motion proposing the sit-in was overwhelmingly carried. That afternoon three hundred students marched up to the Registry and, after some minor scuffles with the porters, entered the building. They swarmed through the offices and corridors, seeking out those empty, carpeted offices in which there would be space to stretch out their sleeping bags. Most of the secretarial staff remained at their typewriters, unperturbed. Meanwhile a committee that had been elected at the Union meeting set about making the necessary arrangements. Food was ordered from a wholesaler in Coventry, a press statement was prepared and a security committee established. Organizationally the sit-in could not have been better.

It soon became clear to the students that in building the Registry, the architects had failed to make provision for any place for holding mass meetings, so amplifiers had to be set up at a convenient point in the corridor. In fact the building is so labyrinthine that on one occasion, when it was felt that the number of occupiers was no more than a few score, a systematic count revealed that there were in fact over two hundred people present. The sit-in passed off very quietly, with little damage. At two o'clock, exactly twenty-four hours after the occupation began, the students departed, leaving behind them a Registry far tidier than it had been at their arrival, and with every file in the place *virgo intacta*.

Six days later the Administration sent out letters to eight of the nine members of the Sit-In Committee, informing them that they were to be charged with 'disorderly conduct in being concerned in breaking into the University Registry on Tuesday 3 February 1970 . . .'. The charge contained certain anomalies. The Vice-President of the Union, who had been a member of the Sit-In Committee, was not charged since he was also a member of the University Disciplinary Committee. Of the eight others charged, at the time of the break-in, two were in the

Union office, one was in Coventry, and one was having a pre-sit-in bath.

On the same day as the announcement of the charges Council made its decision on the social building, and the Vice-Chancellor took the unprecedented step of sending a letter to every student explaining Council's decision and the reasons behind it.

At the Union meeting in the lunch hour on Wednesday 11 February, the students were to discuss the question of disciplinary procedures against the Sit-In Committee, whilst a further meeting was to be held at five to discuss Council's decision on the social building. That morning the President and the President-Elect, both named in the disciplinary charges, had had a meeting with the Advisory Committee of Senate, the body responsible for laying the charges. The result of this meeting was now contained in a sealed envelope that the President, with a rare sense of the dramatic, held in his hand at the start of the meeting. There must have been over five hundred people crowded into the 'Airport Lounge', the main meeting area in Rootes Hall. There was a feeling of great indignation at the Administration's action in bringing disciplinary charges against an elected Union committee. If the contents of the envelope revealed that the charges were to be pressed, then some form of direct action would be the inevitable consequence of such a mood. The President opened the envelope and read: 'In the light of information received this morning, the University has decided not to proceed ...'. The Administration had backed down. However, the situation was somewhat more complex; the timing of the charges was necessarily linked with Council's decision on the social building. Had the Vice-Chancellor intended to use the charges to intimidate the students from further direct action? If so, then he had sadly miscalculated, for fundamental issues had been raised which could not be satisfied by a mere retraction of the charges. Something more positive was demanded.

Instead of dispersing and reconvening at five, the students decided to discuss their attitude to Council's decision on the social building without delay. It appeared that in effect Council had offered the students some form of compromise. Yet

Council's failure to deal with the crucial question of control, and the current mood of the student body, created an atmosphere that was conducive to the idea of the reoccupation of the Registry, not as before on a token basis but indefinitely -- until the University Council gave a decision on the social building which was acceptable to the students. Prior to the Council meeting, the students had demanded either a totally integrated staff/student building or an autonomous Union building. But in the circumstances that were developing, compromise seemed unacceptable. The students were not now prepared to accept a segregated students' building. The notion of an academic community, they felt, required that staff and students, as well as working together, should also relax together. The motion to reoccupy the Registry was passed, although there were some who felt that the tactic of reoccupation was unimaginative and would be ineffective.

So again the faithful three hundred embarked upon the half-mile trek through the Warwickshire countryside. A few hastily gathered red flags fluttered at the head of the march as it snaked its way up Gibbet Hill to the Registry.

Entering the building unimpeded, the students found that the majority of offices were still occupied, and those that were not had been locked. Students gathered around the office doors and encouraged the secretarial staff to leave, provided they left their offices unlocked. There were no secret plans at this stage for a thorough search of the Registry; quite simply, the offices were carpeted and warm and therefore reasonable places for sleeping in.

Sir Walter Coutts, the Assistant Vice-Chancellor, was concerned about the welfare of the secretarial staff; taking aside three of the less militant members of the Sit-In Committee, he agreed to open all the offices as long as no damage occurred. This was put to the sit-in and accepted. Within a matter of minutes all staff had left, leaving unlocked doors behind them.

The atmosphere on this occasion was far less festive. The novelty of occupying the Registry had worn off, and there was also a genuine fear that the police might be brought in; lookouts were posted along the road leading to the Registry, and entrances were barricaded with tables and chairs. This time the students were there to stay.

With the non-appearance of the police the tension relaxed. The 'normal' administrative functions of a sit-in were undertaken, and in fact many students began drifting off to lectures or seminars.

At about eight o'clock that evening, one of the students (in an office next to the Vice-Chancellor's) began thumbing through a file marked 'Student–University Relations', which had not been locked away. Amongst other things the file contained a report from a certain Mr Catchpole on a meeting addressed by Dr David Montgomery, an American Labour Historian who had been visiting the University the previous year. The student thought that perhaps Edward Thompson, who had been a colleague of Montgomery's, might be interested in hearing the contents of the report. The student phoned him. By the time Thompson had arrived at the Registry, the contents of the report and the covering letter from Gilbert Hunt (see pp. 106–8) were being read to the assembled two hundred students. The students were stunned and very angry. Thompson interrupted the meeting and asked permission to take the documents away to have them reproduced and distributed to every member of staff by the following morning. After Thompson's departure the students continued to debate whether or not they should undertake a systematic search of all the files in the building. No one believed that the Montgomery documentation was not incriminating and unjustifiable; the only issue at stake was whether or not the guarantee obtained by Coutts that there should be no damage was still valid. Finally it was decided that a search had to take place but that a minimum of physical force would be employed. This was to be no rampage. Filing cabinets were to be opened systematically, their contents examined, and carefully selected material photo-copied and then returned to the relevant file. The students were outraged, but above all determined. These feelings were exacerbated even further by two rather painful memories. Firstly there was the assurance given on two separate occasions by the Administration that no political information was kept, and secondly there was the memory of porters removing files when the students had arrived at the Registry earlier that day.

The picture was an incongruous one. The well-appointed offices of the Vice-Chancellor and his Assistant were crammed full of students, earnestly reading through files with a pile on their left of what was still to be read and a pile on their right of 'completed work'. Assiduously they read page after page of correspondence, reports, minutes, etc. One student was in charge of every group of 'readers'; each group was allotted to a particular cabinet, and when one of the readers discovered something he considered important it was handed to the student in charge. If the information was relevant it was then taken to be photo-copied and collated. The shortcoming of this system was the lack of coordination between students working on different sets of files; information that seemed harmless enough in isolation might have been of some significance had it been linked with information that was being revealed elsewhere. For example, the fact that the University had been constantly receiving information from the Warwickshire Constabulary about every minor offence involving Warwick students did not at the time seem of great import, but had it been related to the general picture of surveillance that students elsewhere were revealing, it might have appeared in a very different light.

These were the simple mechanics of the operation. The existential nature of the experience involved, however, defies simple description. The enormity of what the students were doing would suddenly strike home. They would be engulfed by the feeling either that this just was not real, or that the consequences of what they were doing were going to be so far-reaching that they would be totally overwhelmed by the force of events. In the room containing the personal files, students were unearthing the confidential reports sent by their headmasters when they had applied to Warwick: 'A fine run-getter in House cricket' and 'A good little mimic' were two of the remarks the headmasters had considered relevant. On discovering the trivial nature of these personal files, the students decided not to search them.

News from the Registry spread through the University the following morning. A crowd gathered in the Airport Lounge at lunchtime. The President was angry – he had given his word to Coutts and it had been broken. The students from the Registry were also angry, because, despite the revelations, there were still many that did not feel that breaking into the files was fully justified. In the middle of the discussion a girl rushed into the Airport Lounge: 'The French Department has come out on strike over the political files issue.' The effect of this announcement was electrifying; the meeting broke up, people rushed down to the teaching block to convene departmental meetings. This was without precedent; never before had members of the University gathered into departments to discuss matters not directly related to academic pursuits. The atmosphere in these joint staff–student meetings was intense; motions were passed calling on the University to destroy its political files, to institute a public inquiry – some even called on Butterworth to resign. News of these meetings spread rapidly across the campus, and was phoned through to the students in the Registry: the University was seething.

To the staff, the only information available was that sent out by Thompson, and many did not consider this as proof. Students who had been in the Registry quoted from memory evidence they had come across. 'Show us the proof,' demanded the more obstinate members of the staff. 'Come to the Registry,' replied the students. Thus the dilemma of the evidence began.

On this same day, Thursday 12 February, a mass meeting of staff and students was called for five o'clock in the Airport Lounge. Never in the history of the University had so many of its members gathered together in one place, and only then did they realize that the University provided nowhere suitable for such meetings of over a thousand of its members. If ever there was a moment of birth of Warwick University, it was at that meeting. A University is not born when the Privy Council grants it a charter; it is born when its members come to realize that they have common interests and a common identity. At that meeting students and staff, who were present in great numbers, began to realize just that. Documents from the Registry were read to the meeting. They included a further case of political spying, and the refusal of an applicant on political grounds. Edward Thompson condemned in the strongest possible terms the keeping of political files. He called on the members of the academic community to reassert themselves, and warned of the dangers of an indiscriminate wave of repression emanating from the Administration. Until then most staff and students had been thinking in terms of 'Warwick's own bit of student protest'. But now they realized that a challenge was being made to the whole structure of the University, and in particular a challenge to the power vested in the industrialists to control the lives of staff and students alike. The major decision taken by this vast meeting was that the sit-in should be terminated, since now the whole nature of the debate had been changed and the negotiating strength that the occupation gave to the students was no longer relevant – there was nothing to negotiate about.

Meanwhile, back in the Registry, the systematic examination of the files had continued all day and the evidence was mounting, but it was as yet far from complete. At about 8.45 pm an emissary arrived from the mass meeting. The occupiers were understandably irate when they were informed that the body of students half a mile away in Rootes Hall had decided that they should leave. If they were going to evacuate it was to be their decision and no one else's. At ten o'clock five hundred students marched up to the Registry, intending to announce their solidarity with the occupation, but to call for its immediate suspension. Instead, a meeting was convened in the snow outside, at which the issues were again thrashed out. The students working in the Registry claimed that much was still to be done, and mainly because of this the meeting, by a narrow majority, extended the time of occupation until ten o'clock the following morning.

The meeting terminated and the serious work of data collection proceeded. At 11.30 that evening the students in the Registry were interrupted by the sound of a loud-hailer outside: '... upon hearing Counsel for the Plaintiffs *ex parte* it is ordered that the defendants . . .'. The students rushed to the upstairs windows and saw below four legal-looking gentlemen, standing together, one of whom was reading an injunction (see p. 131) into a microphone, one aiming a loud-hailer at the Registry, and the other two shining torches on to the injunction.

Reading an injunction in the dark was obviously a most complex and skilled operation. In the far background Butterworth, the Registrar and the Assistant Vice-Chancellor were dimly seen.

As soon as the injunction had been served, the students acted. Copies of the injunction were circulated around the halls of residence, legal advice was obtained, and the University files (being conveniently at hand) were consulted to find the addresses of those who were enjoined but not present. There were twenty-one names on the injunction – of these, four had played no part in the sit-in, seven were well-known 'moderates', one was a member of the Monday Club, and one, Sue Armstrong, did not exist!

Earlier in the evening a meeting had been arranged for 10.30 the following morning. The news of the injunction spread rapidly and as the time for the meeting drew near it was estimated that there were twelve hundred students and staff crammed into the Airport Lounge. The lawyers were undecided as to whether or not the injunction was a blanket. The students had complied with it up to a point by leaving the Registry at nine instead of ten, but they were determined not to be intimidated and to publish all the information found in the Registry. The meeting called for an independent public inquiry into the whole administration of the University, and elected a Committee of Seven to be responsible for directing all further action. The committee which the students elected included a majority of known socialists, together with 'hard liberals'; it was a committee composed of people whom the students trusted to execute policies which might be hazardous and could involve conflict, not only with the University but also with the law. Hopefully this committee would also link up with a committee that the staff would elect at an informal meeting called for that afternoon. The mood of the morning meeting was optimistic, especially as it was hinted that as long as the students acted 'sensibly', then the staff at their meeting were likely to swing *en masse* behind them. With this aim in mind the students acted with restraint; indeed, all they did was to call for the inquiry.

The students awaited the results of the staff meeting. Late that afternoon, as the staff returned from their meeting, the

news sounded depressing. Apparently, after attempts to prevent the meeting from taking place had been thwarted and
after only an hour's discussion, the staff had deplored the
keeping of political records (see p. 125), but had refused to
join the call for a public inquiry and to elect a committee to
work with the Committee of Seven. The student meeting reconvened that evening; in marked contrast to the buoyancy of
the morning gathering, there was an air of depression. Thompson's warnings about the wave of repression felt ominously
real, and now, despite efforts to cement a staff/student alliance, the students were isolated. But they decided to continue
their efforts to uncover the truth about the University Administration.

The following day, Saturday, Senate met at 10 am. Their
meeting ended at 7.30 that evening and a statement was issued
on Sunday night. The statement (see p. 126) supported the
injunction and indicated that internal disciplinary action was
to be taken. Senate also announced their decision to invite
Lord Radcliffe to inquire into the procedures adopted *vis-à-vis*
the retention of political information. In seeking to present
their case in the best possible light Senate took three unprecedented steps. Firstly, their statement was distributed to all
members of the University; secondly, the newly discovered
body, the departmental meeting, was to be reconvened; and
thirdly, Senate invited itself along to the student meeting
scheduled for 6 pm that Monday evening. It was not without
significance that only at this moment of crisis did Senate as a
body deign to communicate with the mass of students.

'A Selection of Documents Extracted from the Registry Files'
was the title of a dossier that appeared on Monday morning.
Throughout the weekend members of the University had
worked to produce this twenty-page document (most of the
contents are reproduced in the documentation section of this
book). By Monday it had been distributed to all staff and
students, as well as to the Press and to other universities, in
spite of the High Court injunction. The operation had been
undertaken in a tense, clandestine atmosphere in which every
lamp-post had to be regarded as a 'Catchpole in disguise'.

In the departmental meetings called by Senate for that afternoon, disbelieving academics were no longer able to say, 'Show us the evidence.' It had arrived by their morning mail and there was nothing they could do about it. Yet still they refused to discuss the documents, for now all the evidence, they claimed, was *sub judice* until Radcliffe had reported: this was 'Catch-22' with a vengeance! The main discussion of these meetings revolved around the Senate's statement of the previous day. 'How can the inquiry be independent when Radcliffe is Chancellor?' demanded the students. 'The Chancellor is only a titular position,' replied Senate. This dialogue – unresolved – continued for hours.

That evening over one thousand staff and students gathered together for yet another meeting. Senate, including the Vice-Chancellor, arrived as a body. Reports from departmental meetings were heard, several calling for the Vice-Chancellor's suspension. Professor Hugh Clegg stood up on behalf of Senate to defend their statement. It was a shrewd move, for Clegg was a known liberal and not unpopular with the students; would he be able to placate them? Clegg was listened to in polite silence. He began by talking about Senate's concern over the state of the University, and how it was determined to improve the social and academic atmosphere. Only later did he broach the subjects of Radcliffe and then discipline. He sat down. Questions were asked which became increasingly hostile as the anger of the students resurfaced. Senate had failed to defuse the situation, and senators left the meeting looking even more worried than when they had entered.

After Senate's departure the meeting relaxed somewhat. A series of motions was passed (see p. 127) which included a rejection of the Senate's statement. During the debate on these motions Professor David Epstein, who until then had not been conspicuous on the students' side, rose to speak. With much deliberation he read his speech. The impact was dramatic. The meeting, which had been in progress for three hours, was flagging. As Epstein spoke it came together. It was apparent that what he was saying was of great moment (see p. 128). The speech was short but the effect was profound. He received a standing ovation.

On the following day the *Birmingham Post*, undeterred by

the injunction, led on the headline 'Boy Turned Down after Head's Letter, Students Claim'. This was the first major breach in the wall of silence erected by the injunction. Just at the time when the student body was again feeling isolated, much-needed outside support began to rally. Apart from the Press and other universities, MPs and trade unionists took an interest in the events at Warwick, for the disclosures that local industry had been spying on its workers outside working hours were of national concern.

On this same Tuesday notices from Lord Radcliffe were circulated around the University (p. 130). They were an invitation to submit evidence to him, on the limited subject of the procedures adopted by the University for the receiving and retaining of political information. At this stage the students were in two minds as to how far they should collaborate with Radcliffe. They objected to his imposition of secrecy, they felt that his terms of reference were too narrow, and most of all they failed to see how the Chancellor of the University could be in any sense of the word 'independent'. Senate, meeting the following day, made some gestures in the student direction by asking Radcliffe to accept two independent assessors, which he refused, and by extending his terms of reference to include other allegations of improper administrative conduct. The students, although uncertain about the independence of the Chancellor, subsequently decided with reluctance that evidence would be submitted.

After the discovery of the files at Warwick, the issue took on national proportions. Warwick students adopted two additional tactics for pushing their case further. Firstly, they held a mass lobby of Parliament on Thursday 5 March. (In response to this lobby, on 18 March some fifty Labour and Liberal MPs signed a motion calling for a public inquiry into the University's affairs.) Secondly, they extended the term for a week, for the purpose of running an 'Open University'. This has involved lectures, seminars and dances open to all, and in particular open to the people of Warwickshire, whom the University was originally intended to benefit. The extension of the term also embarrassed the Administration by jeopardizing the organization of conferences at the University during the vacation.

Students have often felt that Rootes Hall had been designed primarily as a conference centre, and only secondly and incidentally as a social building for an academic community.

The struggle at Warwick had begun over this issue of the social building; after the discovery of the files attention was focused on the propriety of keeping political information; in the weeks following the issues changed. The students began to realize that these were not the real issues at all, but were merely symptoms. What was wrong was the whole concept and structure of the University. The ideals of academic excellence and the pursuit of knowledge had to be reasserted over the aims of the 'Business University'. With this end in mind the students began campaigning for a change in the structure of Council; the oligarchic rule of the Midland industrialists would have to be ended. Students demanded the suspension of the Vice-Chancellor and Gilbert Hunt. They set to work on a new democratic Charter for the University, to be submitted to the Privy Council.

These events had transformed the atmosphere and environment of the University. In these few hectic weeks there was but one topic of conversation; every move in the struggle was closely followed by staff and students alike. The University of Warwick only began to find its identity in a time of crisis. Perhaps this was an inevitable outcome of the original conception of the University as a 'Mid-Atlantic Business School' of twenty thousand; but if all this new-found identity achieves is the prevention of the realization of this scheme, then its achievement will have been great indeed.

Chapter 3
Three Aspects of 'The System'

The Union Building Saga

In the brave new discipline of Business Studies so well developed at Warwick, the theories of Decision-Making and Control in Organizations must surely have the status of exact sciences. But this is not the impression you would get from asking anyone who has tried to understand these processes in action at Warwick. Time and again, after some inept or arbitrary action by what we vaguely think of as 'the Authorities' or 'the Administration', we have tried to find out precisely who was responsible or how the decision was arrived at, only to find that the University discourages research of this kind when it does not come accompanied by large grants from respectable business sponsors. Individuals hide behind committees, and everything we might wish to examine is marked 'Confidential'.

Fortunately now we have managed to get a look at those confidential files, and a few hard facts begin to emerge on which a study might be based. The following is an interim report on our resulting research into who decides what in Warwick, with an accompanying case study: how the Union Building project was repeatedly sabotaged.

A first obvious tension in Warwick, as in most other non-Oxbridge universities, is between academic and non-academic control. The model is a common one, a two-headed oligarchy: the Senate consists of leading academics elected in various more or less indirect ways, and the Council brings together a sub-group of these academics, and the 'lay representatives' who are local notables. The division of powers, on paper, is again the usual one. Senate, flatteringly called in the statutes the 'supreme academic authority' of the University, has control over syllabuses, examinations and student discipline, and advisory powers on staff appointments, while Council has the power of ultimate decision on all questions of finance and equipment (including, what has been most important at Warwick, the buildings), hiring of staff and so on. The principle of 'lay' control ensures a majority of non-academics on Council, divided more or less equally between representatives of local government and other co-opted members.

So far there's nothing unusual -- the systems of government of most universities hardly deserve to be paraded as examples of democratic control. But there are two features in this power structure which are peculiar to Warwick. First, Council is dominated by a group of industrialists who generally support the Vice-Chancellor. Second, when it comes to the crunch, they win.

In fact the Chairman of Council (Hall), the Treasurer (Kerr-Muir), and *eight* of the nine 'co-opted' members belong to the world of business (see p. 31). One can make distinctions among them -- they include both liberals and men of the Right, managing directors with vague academic connexions, and a managing director who is concerned by students distributing leaflets outside his factory. But they have in common their background in industry, and some have a more or less personal relationship with the Vice-Chancellor which does not extend to other members of the University. (Traditionally, the Vice-Chancellor meets the lay members attending a Council meeting -- and no one else -- for lunch immediately before the meeting. With some leading members the relationship is closer than this.) And consequently they have voted with him on a number of crucial occasions, overruling a united academic opposition. Personal friendship, common interests, in particular the financial stake some of them have in the University, has formed them into a group around Butterworth and ensured that Council is likely to be swayed in his favour.

Luckily for him; we know his opinion that 'academics are reluctant to act in a crises [sic]' (see p. 121). So when a conflict with the academics has arisen it has been important in Butterworth's scheme of operation, first, that the lay membership should propel Council in the direction which he favours, and second, that some reason should be found (in a situation where doubt exists) for Council to overrule Senate.

This has happened on at least three important occasions. Each time the question of whose decision was final could be argued on the basis of the statutes, but Senate has failed to contest the fiat of Council. The Union Building decision and the Tyzack Report will be discussed below. In the third contest, Senate had approved the institution of a rotating chairmanship of departments, allowing the post to be occupied by non-professorial staff. On Council, however, the proposal met opposition from the businessmen; in doling out grants for research to science departments, they wanted to be sure of dealing with their peers. So in what was almost self-evidently an academic decision, the 'supreme academic authority' was overruled. The division of powers laid down in the statutes, it has become clear, is subject to *force majeure*; and the union of Butterworth and his friends makes that force.

The handling of the Senate–Council opposition is one way in which the Vice-Chancellor's decisions manage to prevail. But this is not the only place where control is in doubt. Final decisions are rarely deliberated by Council even in quite important cases; this ponderous body is too large and illinformed and meets too infrequently to do more, in most cases, than rubber-stamp a decision already arrived at elsewhere. Senate, suffering from an excess of paperwork and 'final decisions' on trivial cases, similarly tends to delegate authority and accept outside recommendations without debate. And so we find a concentration of power in sub-committees, particularly in Council's Finance and General Purposes Committee (responsible for the allocation of money within the University,* and a vast range of other questions), the Building Committee, and in Senate's Estimates and Grants Committee (see diagram on pp. 10–11). The two Council sub-committees are perhaps the most powerful bodies in the University. But besides control by small and trusted committees, a feature of the system has been confusion of the decision-making process by

---

* The Students' Union grant, for example, is controlled by this committee.

channelling it through a long and arbitrary sequence of committees between which the Vice-Chancellor is normally the only link. At Warwick, the chairman of a committee decides *whether* an item should be placed on the agenda, *where* it should be placed, *whether* a paper for discussion should be circulated; and the draft minutes are generally his responsibility, *not* that of the secretary. The Vice-Chancellor – as chairman of all important Senate sub-committees – and the Registry officials often turn out, in relation to a particular decision, to be the only ones who know where it has come from, where it is to be forwarded to and, most importantly, what changes it has undergone on the way. In a situation where, frequently (examples will be given later), important papers for discussion in a committee appear unannounced on the table at the meeting itself, where inaccurate minutes of a committee meeting circulate as the true record through a number of other committees before they are corrected, where those who are vitally interested in a committee's decisions are not even allowed to know the date on which it will meet – knowledge is power. And the Vice-Chancellor has a near monopoly of the knowledge.

Council, Senate and their sub-committees are where the important decisions are made – decisions which involve money or power or the environment. At a lower level, though, we find the usual purely academic bodies – for example, Boards and Schools of Studies – with a fair degree of autonomy in small-scale decisions on courses, syllabuses, etc.* And, with still less power, there are the 'democratic' bodies of students and staff – Students' Union and Assembly.

The Assembly – on which all academic and Registry staff are entitled to sit – hardly deserves a mention, except that it enjoyed a moment of decisiveness in the Union Building story. It has the right to elect six members to Senate (though not to find out what they are saying) and the right – the only one with

---

*The Vice-Chancellor is Chairman of all three Boards of Studies, but hardly ever attends; the Deputy Chairmanships are powerful academic posts. The only significant appearance of Butterworth at a Board Meeting was to defeat Professor Epstein for the Deputy Chairmanship of the Board of Science, by voting twice – once as chairman. The winner was Professor Clark.

which the statutes are lavish – to 'declare an opinion on any matter whatsoever relating to the University'. Its chairman is, predictably, the Vice-Chancellor, who always attends.

The Students' Union, not mentioned in the statutes, not featured in the flow-chart which the authorities produced to explain their ideas about how decisions were made,* deserves to be taken more seriously. It was at the outset the interest of those in power that student government should be weak and apathetic, and the rapid succession of Union presidents during the first two years, forced repeatedly to resign under pressure from tutors, became a standing joke. The institution of a president with a sabbatical year (which was not lightly conceded) introduced a new period in which the authorities, forced to take seriously the Union's officials, hoped in some way to co-opt them and insulate them from the growing pressure of the mass of students – on the Union Building and a variety of other issues – through a general meeting.

Oscillation between presidents of different kinds – left Labour to Monday Club – meant that this policy met with varying success. The demand that students should be allowed some niche in the University's power structure was often put forward, and this enabled the authorities – as long as the emphasis was on representation rather than control – to play the committee game here as well, temporizing on the scope of representation while conceding student observers at selected meetings, student presence on 'working parties', juggling with liaison committees, and so on. Senate considered the matter of student representation on the governing bodies four times in 1968–9, Council six. After four meetings Council was about to take a final decision to amend statutes in favour of student representation when the Vice-Chancellor decided that the University had not considered the matter 'in depth', and the question was reopened. It is still open. Again the Staff–Student Liaison Committee of Senate has been wound up, probably because it had the audacity to vote on an issue – and the vote went against the Vice-Chancellor.

---

* From that document: 'There is no monolithic administration which "runs the University".'

In contrast to all these manipulations the single most important development at Warwick in the past year has been growing pressure by the Union's membership for more direct democracy as against representation by the small group of union officials, and for the decisions of the increasingly large and politically aware Union General Meetings to be binding on the elected representatives and to determine the course of events.

The Union Building story illustrates what happened when these real people's concern over a real need came into collision with an opaque machine of government run by a group who were completely unable to understand their concern.

In the second autumn of Warwick University's existence, 1966, the main social building, Rootes Hall, was completed and opened to students. Within a month a Union General Meeting was debating the need for a student-controlled Union Building, while the Vice-Chancellor went on record as saying that there would never be a Union Building in the University.

The lines were already drawn. Rootes Hall is a flagrant example of planning from above with no regard for the users. Such planning, such control had been possible in the years preceding the opening of the University. The students hoped to change this system; the Vice-Chancellor intended to see that it stayed intact.

In fact, at this stage the University was committed to a crazy compromise between the Oxbridge college system and a policy of unified social facilities. Students were to be grouped (no one had decided how) into 'Halls', each with about a thousand members, its own administration, catering, accommodation and so forth. Rootes Hall, the monstrosity within which the present students found themselves, was simply the first of these. The second (Jaguar Hall? Sir Arnold Hall?) was to come when the number of students passed the thousand mark. As soon as the demand for a second social building first came forward, the Vice-Chancellor was to claim that the UGC were opposed to a Union Building. They have not confirmed this, and it does not seem to square with the fact that the first development plan, prepared by Coventry's City Architect Ling, included such a building. But the policy was fixed; there was no room for debate. A Union Building had been formally excluded before anyone was there to raise the question.

All the same, the subject had now been raised, and discussion began, at a leisurely pace. At three successive Senate meetings in 1967 the question of a Union Building was on the agenda – as the last item, and so never reached. At two more the Vice-Chancellor got the question referred to the Student Liaison Committee. Council's final decision on the draft plans for the 'Second Hall' was imminent, and Senate had decided nothing, when in November a Union General Meeting voted unanimously in favour of a motion asking for the money allocated to a second hall to be spent on a Union Building instead. Shortly after, the Assembly passed a similar motion by seventy-one votes to thirteen. These motions went before the Council meeting in February 1968.

Professor Zeeman, proposer of the Assembly motion and Head of the Mathematics Department, was a leading advocate of the students' case on Council. However, he had building problems of his own: projected conversions to service an international mathematics research centre were delayed and shunted from one committee to another; finally he received a suggestion that the conversion could start immediately if he dropped his sponsorship of the Union Building. His reply, the first paragraph of which we quote, was unfavourable:

I am most upset by your offer yesterday of the Old Library for Mathematics in return for my laying off the Student Union building. You catch me where I am most vulnerable. You say you do not interfere with my business, why should I interfere with yours? – but student welfare is the business of us all. If I accept this bribe, I foresee that it will impair our respect for each other. It affects not only my own integrity, but also the principle of free speech within the University.

Council met, and rebuked Assembly for expressing an opinion and Zeeman for incorrect practice in circulating its members with the Assembly's decision; rather than go ahead with the second hall, though, and risk opposition (this was 1968, and such possibilities were beginning to be taken into account), Council appointed a working party composed of senior academics, on the whole unsympathetic to the students' case. Already the important shift from Council dealing with the building (as a purely technical matter) to Council arbitrating over the *use* of that building (social policy) had taken place unnoticed. The working party was to report in May – significantly, throughout this story, 'final decisions' have been made at the very end of the academic year in the hope perhaps of escaping a student counter-attack. The party met sixteen times between February and May and produced two plans (not involving a Union Building) for Senate and Council; there were also two plans for a Union Building, one of which came from a Students' Union working party and one from Professors Sargent (Head of the School of Economics) and Zeeman.

The issue was now clearly a matter of the University's social policy. Could a decision of the Senate in this matter be overruled by Council under pressure from the Vice-Chancellor? The senators hoped not and, to give the 'academic view' more force, resolved that their final vote would recommend one of the four alternative proposals *nem. con.* A series of votes led to victory for the Zeeman proposal by thirteen to none. The Students' Union were not entirely happy with this proposal, but accepted that it should go forward to Council.

When Council met, though, there was a carefully organized uncertainty about what Senate had actually decided. The draft minutes mentioned an early unofficial vote (taken on the Vice-Chancellor's initiative) which was not meant to be recorded, and inaccurately gave the impression that the defeated proposal in that vote was for a Union Building. (The minutes were corrected at the next Senate meeting, but the correction did not, apparently, get to Council.) Council was presented (through the reading of the draft minutes) with conflicting accounts of the decisions reached. 'It seems,' commented Sir Arnold Hall, 'that Senate does not know its own mind.' The Senate's vote was not to be taken seriously.

Providentially in any case there was a further reason to kill that Senate decision. At the Senate meeting Butterworth announced that he had 'just received' a letter from Sir John Wolfenden announcing that the UGC could only afford £200,000. This, of course, came at too short notice for the plans submitted to Senate to be revised. Senate's deliberations, therefore, were on a false basis, all previous plans could be ignored, and Council came down in favour of a more modest social building in which 10,000 square feet were to be student run. Two months later the UGC withdrew the money and the whole circus was ready to start again.

From October the University authorities made a great issue of their ignorance about how much money would in the end be released by the UGC; they refused to start discussions with the Students' Union until this was known. February 1969, when the UGC's renewed offer of £200,000 came through, also saw a sit-in in support of the LSE, and the spectre of democracy haunted some professors as two hundred students ended their action with a meal in the staff restaurant. The news of the UGC's offer was not broken to the student representatives until March, when things had quietened down and Senate and Council had appointed yet another committee – the Joint Planning Committee – to discuss the whole question of social facilities. Student representatives were to be allowed to attend meetings of this committee and submit papers to it; the only drawback was that they were not told when the committee was to meet. Indeed, on several occasions, Registry officials refused to reveal the dates of certain meetings, saying that they were acting under instructions. When, in May, the students accidentally got wind of a meeting three days before it took place, prepared papers for it, and turned up, they were told that the papers had arrived too late for consideration and were sent away. Again, these events took place against a background of direct action in the University – the May Day strike. Were the members of the Joint Planning Committee *trying* to prove the futility of constitutional processes and student representation? The lesson took another six months to sink in.

The Joint Planning Committee moved with rapidity, circulating its report to Senate one day before Senate's June meeting. In a similar vein Council, when it met a fortnight later (end of the summer term again), found on the table a *new* report from the Joint Planning Committee, of which the students had not been informed, 'interpreting' the decisions the Senate had just taken. Again, the decisions of the two bodies were opposed: Senate passed by eleven votes to none a motion drawing Council's attention to its previous decisions, and asking for 14,500 square feet to be available for student accommodation, with students participating fully in its planning at all stages. In this, Senate resisted pressure from the Vice-Chancellor to cut back student accommodation in favour of more luxurious staff facilities. Council took the opposite view, and accepted the report of the Joint Planning Committee, providing 10,000 square feet for 3,500 students, compared with 8,000 for a tenth as many staff.

Deadlock once again: Senate was sent to rethink. The penultimate stage of the story saw the reference of the question to a new committee with staff, student and lay members, the Social Policy Committee. This time the existence of a student voice in the discussions seemed at last to offer some promise of a fair deal, and indeed a decision in favour of a joint staff–student building was reached in November with only one dissenting vote.

This dissenting vote was cast by the Pro-Vice-Chancellor, who was Chairman of the Social Policy Committee. As such, he reported to Senate on the committee's decision. Senate then decided, by a majority of only one vote, to opt for a senior common room. The students' participation in the decision process had been useless. Senate had issued an almost open call to direct action.

The lines of discussion in the Union Building story have repeatedly been switched, the terms of debate altered until it seems (a favourite contention of the authorities) that these people – the whole University – do not know their own mind. The situation is carefully contrived to have that appearance. Students have all along known what they wanted – a building for human beings which takes account of their needs as they see them, not as they are determined by those in power; a building which they can administer in their own way, attentive to the requirements of people, not of profit; a place for living in, not a conference centre. Yet these basic needs have been lost in bureaucratic mystification – protracted delays followed by hasty decisions, doubts cast on committee decisions by disputed minutes, lengthy discussions invalidated by reported decisions of government bodies, sub-committees and working parties thrown out in all directions. The students, in playing the committee game for three years, have faced an immensely more experienced and powerful adversary. Now by their own actions they have changed the terms of the conflict, and exposed the manipulations to which the whole University has been subjected.

Academic Policies

How far has the system really produced the kind of University which its industrial promoters wished to see? How far has business influence been actively expressed within the academic policies of the University?

There are no simple answers to these questions. Several factors have worked against any early implementation of the more nightmarish notions of a Business University. Butterworth prided himself, when making his first professorial and senior administrative appointments, in getting 'really good men' – preferably young, ambitious and thrustful – and letting them get on with their own jobs. (The good managing director gives his department chiefs a free hand, provided that they are enhancing the profits and reputation of the firm.) A number of his early appointments *were* 'really good men', and several departments – notably the School of Mathematics – quickly earned a high academic reputation; while the flexibility of a new University, and the enthusiasm of the pioneering staff and students (who felt – what is rarely felt in established institutions – that the University was theirs to make) enabled innovating courses to be founded. In his first Registrar (A. D. Linfoot) the Vice-Chancellor appointed a man who was not only young and exceptionally capable, but also a man of integrity. Linfoot, in his turn, appointed a young and able Registry staff, who kept closely in touch with the academic staff and helped to maintain their first enthusiasm.

Moreover, the early growth of the University was, in terms of the development plan, out of phase. Arts and Social Studies subjects are less costly to found (as is Mathematics), and can more rapidly expand their intake of students, than Engineering and the Physical Sciences. The original plan to have a University in which at least 20 per cent of the students were engineers had to be delayed until a later phase of growth, owing to the inadequate number of applicants from the schools, leaving unfilled places at universities with long-established engineering departments. The Arts (English, History, French, Philosophy) and the Social Studies (Economics, Politics, Law) took up the slack and expanded more rapidly than had been intended. In 1969, 264 first degrees were awarded in these subjects, as against 127 in the Sciences (Mathematics, Molecular Sciences, Engineering, Physics).

In some respects certain of the Sciences and Social Sciences received favoured treatment from the committees of Council: more Chairs, lavish equipment, priority in building plans, etc. Staff and students in the Arts subjects have scarcely resented this, since they appreciate the heavy capital costs of modern scientific laboratories. Very heavy administrative costs have caused more resentment, as has the way in which the library, with a first-rate librarian and staff, has been pinched of funds. Most resented of all has been the obscurity surrounding the University's Foundation Fund.

Butterworth is one of the trustees of the Foundation Fund and doubtless a powerful one. In all these ways – as Trustee, as a member of the Council's Finance and General Purposes Committee (which carves up the annual grant of public (UGC) money between administrative and academic purposes), and as the University's executive fund-raiser through whom all appeals to the major foundations must be channelled – he has been able to exert a commanding influence over an input of some millions of money, some private, but mostly public. Hence his powers to dispense or withhold influence, to divide and to rule, to attach to himself certain professors, expectant of favours for some cherished project, have been enormous.

Not all these favours have been directed towards the Sciences or Industrial and Business Studies. German has its Volkswagen Chair, Politics a Volkswagen Senior Lectureship, while History students have received from an anonymous benefactor the funds for a well-publicized, if academically controversial, exchange term in the United States. Nor is there much indication that earmarked research grants in the Sciences are leading to any serious distortion of academic priorities, although there is a utilitarian tone in the University's self-advertisement which suggests that the problem is present. 'What the university can offer', Professor Shercliff of Engineering told *The Times* technology correspondent, 'is speed in tackling problems';

'running rings round the more ponderous government and research association laboratories', and indeed getting results in many cases faster than industry itself. For firms concerned mainly with immediate sales and profits . . . the University can take a longer-term look ahead ('Science at Warwick University', *The Times*, 10 February 1970).

With work going on in such problems as metal fatigue (Massey-Ferguson), fuel injection system (Rover Company), vehicle instrumentation (Rootes and Ford Motor Company), fatigue in tyres (Dunlop), and high-speed machine-tool cutting tips (Alfred Herbert), one could forecast a danger that some local industrialists might see the University largely as a laboratory for their own research and development.

This problem is, as yet, no more serious than at most universities, and no doubt the Warwick scientists are aware of it. In any case, the greater part of the scientific and technological research grants come directly from the Science Research Council, which has itself given approval to the 'MIT' image of Warwick and to close interrelations of this kind. A Joint Study Group of the UGC and of the University (reporting in November 1966) heard the Vice-Chancellor present evidence that 'the University was determined to produce graduates in engineering, physics and so forth, who were well-adjusted to enter industry'; and that:

The geographical situation of Warwick University, and its existing links with the Motor Industry Research Association . . . suggested to him and his senior colleagues that automobile engineering should be high in the University's priorities.

Both undergraduate and graduate courses should place emphasis on automobile engineering. The Joint Study Group appeared to endorse these statements of intention. Two members of the Science Research Council who visited Warwick in the same year also reported favourably, giving specific support to proposals for graduate training schemes in industry, staff interchange with industry and consultancies, and research contracts with industry. From all such schemes they hoped to see

the production of an increasing number of students who had been educated in a way which a university would regard as satisfactory, but which would enable them to fit more easily and quickly into industrial life (C. Jolliffe to J. B. Butterworth, 29 September 1966).

These encouragements culminated in a meeting on 15 November 1966 between representatives of the University and representatives of the Science Research Council, the Social Science Research Council and the Ministry of Technology, at which more blessings were sought and received. Mr Martindale of the Ministry of Technology said that his Ministry

was interested in the provision of advisory consultancy services, and he hoped that the University would look at any such scheme in a thoroughly commercial manner. Such a service should include a management element as well as a technology bias.

It would therefore be wrong to see the University as being steered in this direction by the plans of the Vice-Chancellor and of a few close Council associates: the direction was being pointed also by the Science Research Council, the Social Science Research Council, the Ministry of Technology, the University Grants Committee and the Institute of Directors. The stage was set for phase two of development, which was signified by Council in February 1967 when it appointed a very powerful selection of its own members to represent it on a Joint Committee on Industrial Studies: these included Hall, Butterworth, Kerr-Muir, Harley, Hunt, Lyons, Mead, Lord Rootes and Young (all officers and 'co-opted' members). In this phase it might seem that the University was running somewhat ahead of any direction which the UGC or any extra-University body had pointed towards; but the story is tangled and our research has not unpicked it all.

The Professor of Business Studies, B. T. Houlden (Operational Research Consultant for NATO and formerly Director of Operational Research with the National Coal Board), first offered proposals for his master's degree course to Senate in June 1966: the course was to be made up of shorter courses in Government and Industry, Quantitative Techniques, Functional Fields of Management, Integrative Studies (management organization, computerized management information systems, strategy planning and business policy) and Human Behaviour –

including the underlying concepts of motivation, learning, etc., the behaviour of individuals and groups, and leading up to industrial relations and management organization from the viewpoint of the social psychologist.

Human Behaviour was later dropped (November 1966). At some point the Institute of Directors' Professor of Business Studies (Houlden), the Pressed Steel Professor of Industrial Relations (Clegg), the Barclays Bank Professor of Management Information Systems (R.I. Tricker) and the Clarkson Professor of Marketing (J. D. Waterworth) were brought together in a single Jumbo Pack as the School of Industrial and Business Studies. Professor Houlden came forward to explain to Senate a general theory of the nature of management, which in 1967 the University's publicity officers were able to reduce to a suave brochure, designed to solicit yet more industrial lolly. The tone was expansive ('our unique situation in the heart of one of the most efficient conurbations in Europe'), and the University was clearly among the most forward-looking of Marketeers:

At a time when Britain is looking forward to entering Europe, and a time when the young in Britain are already European in outlook, the leadership from universities is crucial . . . .

British universities, it asserted,

have traditionally provided training which, whilst excellent in itself, has not developed the type of mental discipline in its graduates needed for the problems which they subsequently face in industry and commerce.

Warwick, it implied, had got its mental disciplines sorted out. Appealing for the funds for two Chairs, to make a Superjumbo Pack – the Chair of Management Information and a Chair of Business Finance – it described with care the austere academic concerns of the latter:

Basic concepts of profitability, risk and uncertainty in relation to investment, the management and evaluation of assets, capital budgeting under certainty, the incidence of taxation, capital replacement decisions. The choice of finance, the new issue market, institutional leaders, leasing, capital gearing and the cost of capital, taxation and company policies, take-overs, long-term financial planning.

An impression has arisen in our research that the UGC, while rushing ardently into Warwick's arms in phase one (the automotive phase) of its planning, was somewhat reluctant to accept its embraces in phase two. In response to inquiries in 1967 from Sir John Wolfenden – and a half-raised eyebrow at first-degree courses in Business Studies – Butterworth hastened to reassure him:

It may be a significant comment ... on our activities that when for instance Mr J. R. Edwards, Managing Director of British Motor Holdings in Birmingham, wishes to reorganize the whole of the industrial relations of his firm, he comes and talks to members of our Industrial and Business Studies Centre rather than anyone nearer home and this is only one isolated instance of what is currently occurring (Butterworth to Wolfenden, 3 August 1967).

As to a first-degree course (restyled as Management Sciences) 'industrialists whom we have consulted about the proposed course have been enthusiastic as soon as the content of the course has been explained to them'.

Whatever reservations Madam UGC may have had, she was very soon a consenting party. Management Sciences were not only authorized, they received a supplementary grant. Meanwhile, repeated appeals by the Board of Arts, the Board of

Social Studies and Senate to the Vice-Chancellor to use his influence with the UGC to lift its arbitrarily low ceiling upon graduate numbers in Arts and Social Sciences at Warwick – a ceiling which was actively damaging academic developments of a promising kind – met with less success. Miraculously, wherever 'industry' was mentioned the governmental or quasi-governmental agencies came up with support; wherever, in the Arts or Social Sciences, the academic staff attempted to press forward along their own natural lines of growth, nothing gave way.

To find out the whole story of this episode the students of Warwick may have to occupy the UGC. Meanwhile, in the coming years Business and Industrial Studies are certainly major growth-areas. The Pressed Steel Professor of Industrial Relations (Clegg), coming to Warwick from the Prices and Incomes Board and the Donovan Commission after the University's teething troubles were over, landed the greatest catch of all: $250,000 from the Ford Foundation, £100,000 from the Leverhulme Trust, and £200,000 from the Social Science Research Council (an unprecedented sum from this source).

No doubt his research plans were well founded, and the support came in tribute to his academic eminence. But, at the same time, the ways in which society asserts its priorities, and in which this or that area of research – management studies or work on racial conflict or criminology or, even, the living theatre – is selected for support by public or by private money, are clearly ones which require less 'confidentiality' and more open examination. And, in the context of the Warwick story, two further points may be made, one trivial, the other of more consequence.

A trivial point concerns the holding of industrial consultancies. Warwick has favoured its staff holding such part-time appointments from early days: an early paper on 'Industry as a Field of Study' declared 'the University would be willing to allow and even to encourage its academic staff to undertake research work on a consultant basis in connexion with business problems'. Industrial consultancies are no more heinous than other forms of part-time outside employment, such as correcting A-level papers or writing articles for *New Society*. But in a situation of adhesive relations with industrial capitalism the holding of consultancies with industrial firms whose directors are also influential members of the University's Council should perhaps – like the business connexions of MPs – be published and declared?

The second point concerns the academic situation of such disciplines as Industrial and Business Studies – not in a period of comparative industrial tranquility, but in a possible situation of acute industrial and political conflict. How are the lecturers and students in such disciplines to be situated if, in a period of conflict, some of them sympathize with and assist the labour movement, and yet the governing Council of the University includes industrialists whose views and interests may conflict with the basic principles of academic freedom? One does not have to be an eminent academic to understand the danger and to know what the reply should be.

Loyalty and Security

So far, in following the working of the system, we have seen astute handling rather than any violent infracture of procedures. A vital question has been the control of the flow of communications: between students, academic staff, and even (on occasion) between Senate and Council, between the University and the UGC and other grant-awarding bodies. In terms of total funds used by the University, grants from industry and other outside sources do not appear to have been of overwhelming importance. In the 1969 accounts the following figures are given:

	Capital expenditure up to 31 March 1969	Income year ending 31 July 1969
Total	£10·67 million	£1·75 million
Of which from non-Treasury sources	£1·3 million	£0·25 million

The bulk of the capital expenditure financed by outside interests is accounted for by the student blocks of residence (£650,000).

This comparatively small injection of private money (itself often subsidized to the tune of 8s 3d in the £ by the taxpayer) can however exercise a disproportionately great influence in terms of general direction of growth. It serves as a lever for indicative planning. Public money not only services the hum-drum academic purposes of the great bulk of the staff and students – those teaching and studying economics or philo-sophy or engineering – it also (together with a part of the *un*-earmarked benefactions in the private appeal fund) provides the infrastructure of buildings and administration for the insti-tution as a whole. Working within this public structure small earmarked funds, placed here and there, can indicate the growth-points and long-term future development of the place. Chairs can be established on terms of a few years' private covenant, under an agreement by which the University under-takes on the expiry of the covenant to take the post on to its normal budget – thereby mortgaging the University's future growth for many years to come. Hence, out of the major terri-tory of hard-working and reputable disciplines, one sees the sudden burgeoning of lavishly supported activity in areas such as Business Studies, whose academic credentials are open to question and whose intellectual or social priority has not been seen to be established by any open democratic process.

In Warwick the business ethos has, however, achieved an unprecedented influence, not so much in indicative planning as in the general attempt to model the University's operations upon the managerial style of a certain kind of business. Butter-worth himself has said at at least one meeting of Assembly: 'We must remember that Council is our employer.'

Such a managerial style necessarily involved him in conflict, not only with students (over such issues as the Union Building) but also with academic staff (who came to Warwick with ex-perience of other more democratic or more formal bureau-cratic traditions) and with his own Registry officials, to whom belonged the first responsibility for ensuring that all formal procedures were correctly observed.

A Vice-Chancellor anxious to reassure 'industry' that he was turning out graduates with the right 'mental discipline' was not likely to prove to be sympathetic to the pressures for greater student and staff participation or control which first became widespread in Britain in 1967. Nor was he. In June 1967 the Pro-Vice-Chancellor, Wilfred Harrison, Professor of Politics, prepared a paper for Senate on 'Communications with Academic Staff and Students': the paper was prepared 'at the request of the Vice-Chancellor', and perhaps included some of his own ideas. The paper indicated, without supporting evidence, that some students and some junior members of staff were deliberately fostering suspicion of the motives of the Administration, and offered suggestions as to how to 'isolate and contain those who are merely agitators'. The paper was received by some Senators with scepticism; no one saw it as a first step in the direction of the establishment of a security system.

More startling was the vigour of the Vice-Chancellor's response to an episode of student activity early in 1969. On 30 January the students called an official strike and demonstration in support of the students at the LSE, which included a march, led by the student President, into Coventry. Against the advice of the Registrars, messages were sent to departments asking for the names of all students absent from lectures or seminars to be noted and sent to the Registry – and adding, for good measure, short lists of names of students about whom information was particularly requested. To their credit, most of the departments refused to supply this information, and several (including Economics and History) circulated official protests. One professor (himself of strongly Conservative politics) was made indignant by telephone inquiries from the Vice-Chancellor as to the whereabouts of one of his lecturers.

If this information was (as one must suppose) being collected and filed, it was not in the normal student record files of the Registry. The tensions here, between Butterworth's line-managerial style and more traditional styles of professional administration, can still only be guessed at. The most eloquent fact is that, by the end of 1969, scarcely more than four years from the first opening of the University, the University had lost the services of its Registrar, Deputy-Registrar, and at least six more senior administrative officials, a turnover which must be without precedent. Moreover, the men and women who left had been respected and trusted by the staff, and were well known for their accessibility and efficiency.

These resignations may have been related at certain points to the handling of procedures which have already been indicated. The crisis of confidence between Butterworth and his Registry arrived when Council commissioned, in November 1967, a firm of industrial consultants, John Tyzack & Partners, to carry out an investigation into the administrative structure of Warwick. Their report was presented in a style, and revealed a manner of thinking, somewhat strange to academics. 'Taken as a whole, the University is certainly inefficient by normal commercial or industrial standards.' Assuming for no stated reason that the University's policy demanded a rapid rate of expansion, it cautiously recommended 'economies' to further this by means of an increase in the ratio of students to staff. (To a university teacher this means more work, or poorer teaching to larger groups; the student's 'economy' is to find staff less available.) The Vice-Chancellor (the report said) was heavily engaged in 'maintaining the momentum' of the University, 'nurturing its reputation for higher academic achievement' and 'fostering its interests in the highest circles, attracting financial support, and enhancing its status by playing a part in the public life of the University world at large both inside and outside the United Kingdom. His image is its image.' He was so busy in these many ways that he required the services of an Assistant or Deputy Vice-Chancellor. This post (it was recommended) should not carry security of tenure: 'the reasoning here is that this is primarily an administrative appointment, and we see no reason why it should not be treated by Council in the same way as a board of directors would treat the appointment of a General Manager.' The University was to be structured according to the principle of absolute loyalty and responsibility to its chief executive, the Vice-Chancellor. The Vice-Chancellor should have the power to veto committee decisions and refer them back to Council or Senate. Indeed, Messrs Tyzack perceived very little to recommend itself in the University's structure of academic policy-making:

We have been told that democracy has a special place in university life, and that there is constant political pressure from the rank and file of the academic staff claiming the right not only to be consulted more but to 'have a hand in decision-making'. The result in practice is already an amorphous and time-wasting system which has led to needlessly protracted argument, dilatoriness in the taking of decisions, uncertainty regarding the effective centres of power and action, and at times to conflicts of policy....

No firm could increase its output in this slovenly way. 'Sooner or later the University of Warwick will have to come to terms with the age-old conflict between democratic principles and effective government.' Indeed, academic committees would not stand up before time-and-motion study. 'Committees absorb not only the energies of salaried members of the academic staff whose primary function is supposed to be teaching and research, but also the time of the Registry staff who have to service the committees. . . . We cannot emphasize too strongly ... that whatever a committee's area of authority it has no power to seek implementation otherwise than through the Vice-Chancellor.'

If committees could not actually be abolished, the smaller the better: 'the bigger the committee the less desirable it is that there should be frequent meetings, for the man-hours consumed will be proportionately higher.'

A section of the report was devoted to the products of this new, forward-looking operation: the students. 'The University must somehow put across the message that the student is considered important as an adult member of the community, and that the authorities care about him and value him.' Representation of students on any important policy-making committees was not recommended: but a student liaison committee might be set up, 'whose main function would be to provide a working link between the students and the Administration rather than the University at large'.

The import of the report was profoundly unsettling to anyone conversant with traditional views of the role and powers of a university Registry. In the view of some of the administrators, the Man from Tyzack had shown insufficient interest in actually finding out what the servicing of academic committees

involved. The Registry was criticized for precisely those services for which the academic staff held it in most respect:

> The chief trouble in the Registry . . . is too many over-serviced
> committees and too much paper. Committee papers are too long,
> too literary, too minutely and academically argued. Minutes are
> unduly loaded with records of what was discussed, and of who said
> what, instead of being statements of decisions reached.

The committee papers 'are models of their kind, beautifully
produced on one side of the paper only [so was the Tyzack
Report], but the model itself is too lavish'. The economies
recommended in the communication flow which a conscien-
tious Registrar and staff had maintained in the face of all
difficulties were more than offset by the cost of the other
Tyzack recommendations. An Administration already expen-
sive was to be supplemented by Assistant Vice-Chancellor,
Steward and other posts. The first post struck at the heart of
the Registrar's traditional status and role in university government.

The Report was presented towards the end of the summer
term in 1968. The Vice-Chancellor was busy in the next month
or two, as his letter to Professor Max Beloff of 8 July confirms.
'We' were also, at this time, 'taking legal advice about tenure
of staff under the University statutes' (see p. 121). (It is not
clear whose 'we' was briefing the lawyers, since Senate had not
been consulted or informed on the matter.) The Tyzack recommendations were not debated until the next academic session.
The events of that debate are unclear, since they include a
meeting of certain Council members and of certain senators
at the London flat of Sir Arnold Hall: the decisions of that
meeting were not minuted. Senate did however minute, on 30
October 1968, its opposition to the main proposals of the
Tyzack Report, by fifteen votes to none. It further passed the
following minute:

> To record that Senate is concerned lest the emphasis on loyalty of
> administrative officers to the Vice-Chancellor in the Tyzack Report

(with which it entirely agrees as a matter of general principle) should inhibit expression of professional opinion, and records its opinion that each officer has a right and duty to express his professional opinion and give all relevant information when asked in Council, Senate or Committee (Senate Minute 493).

Notwithstanding these decisions, Council accepted the main proposals of the Report (on Guy Fawkes Day) on a vote of nine lay members to six academic members, with certain abstentions. Professor Clegg, who had been invited by some Senate members to make a major statement of their case to Council (since he is an authority on consultancy reports), was prevented by another engagement from doing so: he left the Council meeting (through a window, since no other exit was free) before he could speak and before the vote was taken.

This and the Union Building issue indicate the major disagreements between Senate and Council over the University's administrative affairs. The Union decision profoundly disturbed relations between the student body and the rest of the University (see Professor Epstein's statement, p. 128); the second intervention lost the University the services of a dedicated Registrar, his Deputy, and at least two other administrators. It was perhaps to be expected that these would present their resignations, but it is still surprising that Senate and Council should have accepted these without instituting any further inquiry into the cause and, in the case of Senate, without making any serious effort to defend its own officers.

The Tyzack Report has, meanwhile, been implemented by stages. An Assistant Vice-Chancellor (himself in no way responsible for this preceding history) came into office in October 1969. In the same month an attempt to effect a radical restructuring of the Schools of Studies in the Board of Arts, replacing open faculty meetings of the whole staff with small professorial-dominated sub-committees, was resisted only after intense agitation among the Arts lecturers. A new Registrar and Deputy came into office, one or two of whose early actions suggested that they had received from some quarter (and certainly not from the retiring Registrar) extraordinarily misleading briefings as to the trouble-making propensities of some of the academic staff (including senators), and a general brief towards discipline and security-consciousness. Meanwhile, over the past fifteen months (from January 1969 onwards) several attempts have been made to alter the terms of tenure of academic and of administrative staff, attempts which can more readily be understood in the light of the letter from Butterworth to Beloff of 8 July 1968 (p. 120). The first attempts were made on the Finance and General Purposes Committee of Council (20 January and 4 February 1969), when a proposal for redrafting the statutes in ways which would make the dismissal of radical staff more easy was slipped on to the agenda under the heading 'Student Representation on Council'. Only the vigilance of the student observers on Council prevented the item from slipping through unnoticed. Thereafter widespread opposition among the staff – expressed at an Assembly meeting – has prevented the reintroduction of the clause; but similar changes in the security of tenure of senior administrative staff (resisted during the tenure of the previous Registrar) have recently been implemented. The departmental secretaries, telephonists and technical staff have also received a reminder that they work for a loyalty-conscious Business: three weeks after the occupation of the Registry they received a long duplicated document from the Registrar, presented without grace and without thanks for their hard-working service for the University, giving a list of occasions which could result in dismissal, including 'impertinence or insubordination'.

All this has been pretty sick. It has led to the loss of excellent staff, to the withdrawal of several senior academics, of differing political persuasions, from the Senate and from university committees, in various states of disillusion as to the possibility of democratic process. The managerial styling has been informed throughout by insensitivity to or fear of open democratic decision-making and extreme insensitivity to genuine communication – representation and open discussion and debate – between Administration, staff and students. Such questions of human and educational relationship, with the departure of the old Registry officials, have come to be seen increasingly as problems of manipulation or problems of security.

This was how it seemed on the eve of the second occupation of the Registry. It was only then, when the files in the Vice-Chancellor's area were opened, that the full implications of the corporate managerial institution, with its security apparatus, became apparent. What was found there may be indicative only of what might have been found if it had not been hastily removed. (For example, the photographs taken on the demonstration of 30 January 1969, and the names collected of suspect students, did not come to light.) Some of the relevant documents are reproduced at the end of this book, and they require little commentary. It is evident that the security system could extend to the admission of students; to the surveillance of the extra-University activities of students; and to the receipt and filing of information obtained by methods of industrial espionage upon the political and extra-University activities of staff.

Two comments only need be made. The first is that this security system, while evident in all its clear outline, had not yet been fully established, and lay largely within the area of the Vice-Chancellor's personal influence. It was abhorrent, not only to the whole student body, but to the greater part of the staff and to many administrators. Indeed, Butterworth and his close Council allies were still finding it difficult to wrest the academic structures into a managerial style. At the weekly meeting of the (senior administrative) officers not long before the sit-in, Butterworth was still looking for procedures to limit the open discussion of major areas of policy:

The VC said that the laymen on Council and its committees were not pleased when past decisions were reconsidered, as in the case of social policy. In this connexion, he suggested that the recommendations of the Social Policy Committee [a joint committee of Council, Senate and students, set up under the recommendations of the Tyzack Report] should be made direct to the Building Committee or Finance Committee [both committees of Council only] as appropriate, rather than through the Senate, where Senate was not directly concerned.

The second comment is to indicate, once again, the area of most acute sensitivity which – so far as available documents show – informed the actions of at least one leading member of Council. The Aliens Restriction Act which (Hunt to Butterworth, 18 March 1969, see p. 106) was apparently under discussion in the case of Professor Montgomery provided (in the words of Professor Wedderburn) that any alien who

'promotes or attempts to promote industrial unrest in any industry in which he has not been bona fide engaged for at least two years', commits a crime punishable by three months' imprisonment. This xenophobic guard against foreign agitators [continues Professor Wedderburn], posted two years after the Russian Revolution, still slumbers in the statute book (*The Worker and the Law*, 1965, p. 266).

It would seem that someone (Mr Gilbert Hunt?) had been thinking of rousing it from its fifty-year slumbers. And why? Perhaps because Professor Montgomery was the kind of man who did not have the 'mental discipline' of which industrialists approved. A distinguished historian, the author of *Beyond Equality* (1967), he had previously worked for some years in industry in the United States, as a machinist on the shop-floor in the engineering industry, before becoming a university teacher. (It was precisely this unusual blend of academic excellence and practical experience which led advisers in the United States to recommend him to Warwick as the first holder of the American Council of Learned Societies post of Senior Lecturer in American Labour History.) A few months before the interest of Messrs Hunt and Catchpole was aroused, he had allowed his considerable trade-union experience to be called upon in advising a group of Pakistani workers in Coventry who were on strike and trying to get union recognition. He also agreed to address several meetings of trade unionists, Labour Party members and shop stewards – one or two of which were a good deal larger than the one which Catchpole, Norton and their shorthand writer attended – on the consequences of automation and the problems of measured day-work, as experienced by workers in American industry.

What was apparently obnoxious to certain employers in Coventry was not that Professor Montgomery was too little interested in 'industry', but that he was interested in industry too much. The Vice-Chancellor and certain members of his Council, it would seem, are interested in relations with industry – provided that those relations are of one character only and run only one way.

Chapter 4
Implications for the
Labour Movement

Course, the boss may persuade some poor damn fool,
To go to your meeting and act like a stool,
But you can always tell a stool, boys, that's a fact,
He's got a yellow streak a-running down his back. . . .
('Talking Union', American folk song, c. 1940)

If the revelations of the Warwick files were chiefly concerned
with the disturbing relationship between big business and the
University, then by implication they raised the question of the
place of the labour movement in this relationship. In the long
term, closer ties between the University and the local community, as represented through trade unions, might be one of the
happier results of the disclosures. Their immediate implication
for the labour movement, however, lies in their uncovering of
the continued existence of labour espionage.

From their first inception trade unions have suffered the
attentions of the labour spy. This unwholesome specimen has
at times presented a major peril, more often a minor nuisance,
on occasion an unrecognized affliction.

He constitutes one of the least attractive figures in the whole
industrial landscape. Espionage in general is a sordid business,
though it has acquired a certain false glamour in the context
of James Bond-style melodrama. No such glamour is attached
to espionage when directed against the collective organizations
of working men.

The labour spy attracts revulsion, first, because he offends
our fundamental conceptions of civil liberty. Those who would
justify espionage at international level may suggest the need
for national security against external danger. But the industrial or political spy is a symbol of a society which is *internally*
repressive. The struggle for popular liberties was a long and
bloody one. The right to express opinions freely, without the

fear that they may form the basis of some secret dossier, is one which will not lightly be surrendered.

But trade unionists have more specific reasons for objecting to the labour spy. Industrial relations – while there are areas in which the two sides have interests in common – take place within a framework of conflict: fundamental conflict involving issues of money and also of control. In formulating their objectives and their strategies, each side seeks privacy. Neither party to a negotiation will voluntarily reveal, in advance, the exact point at which he is willing to compromise, for this is to surrender an important element of bargaining power. Management for its part can without difficulty discuss its problems and determine its policies in the privacy of company offices. If, at the same time, management can by surreptitious means observe the private discussions of the trade-union side, it obtains a valuable but morally indefensible advantage.

In addition, such espionage is feared as a means of direct assault on trade unionism itself. Who attends the meetings? Who voices grievances? Who proposes action? For a ruthless management such information can form the basis for discrimination against the active unionist, typically in the form of dismissal and the blacklist. It was no accident that the prominent shop stewards of the First World War became the unemployed leaders of the 1920s.

Labour espionage has a long history. In America, for instance, in the 1930s – when the workers' right to organize was in theory guaranteed by the New Deal legislation – such anti-union activities were increasingly perceived as a public scandal. In June 1936 a special inquiry was authorized by Congress under Robert La Follette, a progressive senator. Its terms of reference – 'to make an investigation of violations of the rights of free speech and assembly and undue interference with the right of labor to organize and bargain collectively' – constituted 'the broadest mandate for a civil liberties investigation in the history of the United States' (J. S. Auerbach, *Labor and Liberty: The La Follette Committee and the New Deal*, 1966, p. 73). In more than two years of public hearings, the La Follette committee accumulated dramatic evidence of the extremes to which the major American companies were prepared to take their resistance to union organization: victimizing and blacklisting members, hiring thugs to intimidate, beat up and murder activists, employing professional strike-breakers, even maintaining private armies with arsenals of machine guns and poison gas.

A large proportion of the committee's time was devoted to the activities of the spy agencies. Not surprisingly, the inquiries met extreme opposition.

The people who knew most about it wouldn't talk. They were very secretive. They destroyed many of their records. Often they didn't hear the question – or when they did hear it, they didn't understand it. They beat around the bush. They were shifty, unwilling witnesses. They lied frequently. Nevertheless, there were times when the evidence was so overwhelming that they had to come clean . . . (L. Huberman, *The Labor Spy Racket*, 1938, p. 19).

Some of the most revealing findings related to the Corporations Auxiliary Company, the agency second in importance only to Pinkerton's itself. Its principal customer, the Chrysler Corporation, was found to have paid $76,411.81 in a single year for espionage services. In addition, Chrysler was a leading member of the National Metal Trades Association, which allocated the bulk of its funds to spies and union-breakers. The money paid ample dividends: Chrysler gained detailed reports of the business discussed at United Autmobile Workers meetings at all its plants; for many years it succeeded, through the most brutal methods, in blocking the workers' efforts to organize.

All this is history. What relevance has it to the processes of industrial relations which operate today? It is a commonplace that all important companies have come to terms with trade unionism: a 'mature' bargaining relationship has evolved in which each side is ready to behave 'responsibly', conscious of and sympathetic to the problems which the other faces. Labour espionage was a feature of the bad old days when employers saw unionism as a dangerous enemy, to be resisted by all means, fair and foul, as the necessary tactics of industrial warfare. It formed part of an antediluvian management strategy, now happily extinct. The change in the last quarter of a century has been succinctly described by an American author:

Instead of employing spies through detective agencies, as was done in the 1920s, employers now hired suave persons who called themselves 'industrial relations consultants' (F. Peterson, *American Labor Unions: What They Are and How They Work*, 1963 edn, p. 125).

And yet. . . . The documents discovered by chance in the Warwick files show beyond doubt that the labour spy is alive and well and active in the Midlands motor industry. 'We sent a representative to the meeting on 3 February, at Coundon Road [the Labour Party headquarters],' writes the Deputy Managing Director of Automotive Products Ltd. 'At my request, Mr N. P. Catchpole, our Director of Legal Affairs, attended a meeting of Coventry Labour Party on 3 March', writes Gilbert Hunt, Managing Director of Rootes Motors. And nobody can accuse Rootes Motors of half-measures: with Mr Catchpole went ex-Police Superintendent Norton, Chief Security Officer at the company's Stoke (Coventry) works, together with his shorthand writer.

Exceptional occurrences? Many trade unionists do not think so. For example Hugh Scanlon, President of the Amalgamated Union of Engineering and Foundry Workers, was reported by *The Times* to have the following reaction to the Warwick revelations:

The students' battle for freedom of expression showed that they were just beginning to learn what he already knew. Records were kept of every militant on the shop floor (2 February 1970).

Mr William Lapworth, Coventry District Secretary of the Transport and General Workers Union, was surprised only that company espionage was shown to extend beyond the activities of trade unionists to those of sympathetic academics. He was convinced that the Warwick disclosures were 'just the tip of the iceberg'. One local firm, he alleged,

would spend unlimited sums of money on sending paid representatives to attend meetings. It just shows to what great lengths management will go to find out what their workers are doing, and just what we have been up against. Management try to project an image of themselves as lilywhites, but we know differently.

One particular firm, Mr Lapworth claimed, had kept abreast of technological progress by concealing tape recorders in order to eavesdrop on workers' meetings (*Coventry Evening Telegraph*, 18 February 1970).

Why then this apparent revival of labour espionage? The answer must lie in the wider trends in British industrial relations which have been the subject of so much recent comment. The 'mature' processes of collective bargaining characteristic of the post-war years rested on a novel situation of relatively full employment. The economic environment facilitated strong organization. Trade unions, in other words, had become harder to defeat; while employers who yielded to this fact quickly discovered the unions' value as 'managers of discontent'.* Progressive companies were quick to embrace the union as a partner, guaranteeing a stable, predictable and relatively contented labour force at the cost of modest annual improvements in wages and conditions. Trade unionists, by and large, were only too happy to accept the limits of 'moderation' which were the price of managerial goodwill.

Today the foundations of this cosy partnership seem far less solid than a decade ago. The most dramatic threat to stable relationships stems from the challenge from below: the rapid growth of shop-floor organization, wage drift, unofficial strikes. Britain, so the Royal Commission on Trade Unions reported, has developed 'two systems of industrial relations'; and it is the 'informal system', increasingly, which really matters. As Mrs Castle insisted to the Institute of Directors, power has 'returned to the grass roots whence it came' (*Financial Times*, 7 November 1969).

For some writers this accelerating process is symptomatic of the breakdown of traditional normative restraints in industrial relations (A. Fox and A. Flanders, 'The Reform of Collective Barganing: From Donovan to Durkheim', *British Journal of Industrial Relations*, 1969). At the very centre of this breakdown stands the shop steward. No matter that, according to Donovan, he functions as 'more of a lubricant than an ir-

---

*This perceptive description was coined by C. Wright Mills, *New Men of Power* (1948), p. 9.

ritant' (Royal Commission on Trade Unions and Employers' Associations, *Report*, 1968, p. 29). For British shop stewards have come in for almost unprecedented vilification as wildcats, subversives and wreckers. Almost unprecedented – but not entirely so. Virtually identical language has been used in the past to denigrate the *official* trade-union organization. The intention is usually self-evident: once union activists are defined as beyond the pale, the use of espionage and similar techniques becomes far easier to justify. As one American spy agency assured its 'operatives' in the 1930s:

Remember we are unalterably opposed to all cliques, radicalists and disturbing elements who try to create discontentment, suspicion and unfriendliness on the part of the workers toward the employer . . . (L. Huberman, *The Labor Spy Racket*, 1938, p. 107).

In the 1800s it was the 'Jacobins'; in the 1930s the 'radicalists'; today it is the 'wildcats' and the 'subversive students'; and the response, it would appear, is in each case the same.

A second development, associated with the growing self-assurance of workers' shop-floor organization, is the shift of attitude discernible in official trade unionism. In the past many an officer at the bargaining table has cherished the role of plenipotentiary; such a stance is becoming increasingly less viable. At the same time the self-imposed restraints in pay negotiations are beginning to lose their force: aspirations have become suddenly heightened. Leadership elections in some unions – notably in the TGWU and the AEF – are recognized as a turn to the Left. The general impression is of the hasty exercise of creaking joints as union leaderships strive to reduce the distance between themselves and the rank and file. The transformation in official trade unionism should not, perhaps, be exaggerated – but it commonly is. And the epithets until recently flung only at unofficial militants are now increasingly extended to their national leaders. It would be scarcely surprising, therefore, if the official institutions of the labour movement were to become fair game for espionage.

Yet it is not only changes on the union side which are threatening to undermine the *entente cordiale*. For there is a new aggressiveness apparent within the ranks of management

– an aggressiveness strongly associated with the extension of American ownership within British industry. The Roberts-Arundel affair of three years ago would seem to have set a precedent: an escalating intolerance on the part of American directors towards British unionism's traditional restrictions on 'managerial prerogatives'. In this context it seems more than coincidence that it was the Managing Director of Rootes who sent his spies to report on Dr Montgomery (and also to note whether any of the company's own employees were at the meeting); that Rootes is now controlled by the Chrysler Corporation of America; and that it was Chrysler that spent over $270,000 on labour espionage in the four years 1933–6. Small wonder that Mr William Wilson, MP for Coventry South, told the Press that:

I have already been contacted by members of Rootes staff asking the pertinent question that if this sort of investigation has been carried out on a member of the staff of the University, is it not possible that similar investigations have been carried out on many of those working for the Rootes Group (*Birmingham Post*, 16 February 1970).

The trend towards a revival of labour espionage, dramatically exposed by the Warwick students, presents a serious threat to the whole labour movement. Happily, the response of the movement itself in recent weeks – through its shop-steward committees, trade-union officials and constituency parties – shows a growing recognition of these dangers. On 10 March 1970 the Labour group on the Coventry City Council formally moved that the city's annual grant to the University be withheld until its governing Council had been reformed and made more representative of the life of the City.

Chapter 5
Injunctions and the Press

At about 11.30 pm on Thursday 12 February 1970 a number of men, including some senior University officials, arrived outside the occupied Registry. One man read through a loud-hailer the terms of a court injunction that had been obtained by the University, and a copy was handed to the students within.

Technically, an interim injunction, as this was, is a step in a civil action by which, pending the determination at a full trial of the plaintiff's claim, the court can order the defendants to suspend any activities which interfere with the rights the plaintiff is claiming. The injunction is obtained *ex parte*, that is to say on an application by the plaintiff without the defendant being present. Although it is a civil remedy, breach of an injunction is punishable as a contempt of court, by warning, fines or imprisonment without limitation. As it is clearly quite a serious matter to issue a court order backed by such sanctions in the absence of the defendant, it is normally granted only for a short time, until the defendant can be summoned to a hearing when the judge can decide, after hearing arguments, whether to continue it.

There are clearly some difficulties about using this, or indeed any civil legal procedure, in a situation such as a sit-in. Not only must defendants be named (which often causes aloof authorities some difficulty), but the normal procedure requires service on each of them of a copy of the court order. This is an important requirement if they are to be held in contempt of court for any breach of the order, and personal service can only be waived if evidence is given to the court that such service is impractical. As the *Observer* stated knowingly in relation to the Warwick injunction:

It is very difficult to make an injunction stick. You have to go before a judge in chambers, having sworn affidavits naming the culprits, secure from him writs and serve them personally on each of the individuals named (1 March 1970).

However, High Court judges are becoming increasingly concerned at the 'threat to law and order' posed by the occupation of buildings by squatters and students, where the police are reluctant to intervene, as no breaches of the criminal law are usually involved.

The Warwick Administration therefore had little apparent difficulty in obtaining and serving the injunction within thirty-six hours of the start of the sit-in, and within twenty-four hours of the discovery of the first documents. The University Council had delegated its powers to its Finance and General Purposes Committee, in anticipation of the need to apply for an injunction. The terms of the order were drafted by the University's lawyers, the large City of London corporate solicitors Linklaters & Paines; a Divorce judge sitting on Assize in Birmingham hurriedly approved it, with minor amendments, and gave leave for substituted service by loud-hailer. The injunction was not limited in time and gave no return date for a hearing at which both parties could be present. No writ stating the actual nature of the plaintiff's claim had been issued, and although the granting of the injunction was conditional on issuance of a writ, the writ was not required to be served on the students. In fact, the solicitors had no instructions from the University authorities to serve it at any stage, so that the defendants were never told and could not find out the basis of the University's claim.

In this hasty manner, with no opportunity to argue the issue, a court order of indeterminate scope, backed by the sanction of imprisonment, was applied to the confrontation between members of the University and some of its officers.

According to the statement of 16 February, signed by a number of members of the University Senate, the injunction was obtained 'as a first priority to restoring normal working order'. However, its major impact was in restricting publication of the documents, since the students had decided before service of the injunction to end the sit-in at 10 am on Friday 13 February. It is difficult to estimate what effect the injunction would have had if this decision had not already been taken. Its terms required only the named students to leave the Registry – this particular provision did not (and could not, being a positive order) apply to anyone else. In this respect the injunction differed from the legal weapon used against squatters, which is a writ of possession, which can be used to clear a building of all trespassers. However, the technical scope is probably less important in such a situation than the political effect. Where the determination behind an action such as an occupation is wavering, any court order, whatever its technical nature, could have a decisive effect. However, the effect is not easily predictable, as the University authorities at Manchester discovered, when an injunction issued to try to prevent a few students from 'inducing or counselling or inciting' others to sit-in had the effect of snowballing support for a sit-in.

The remaining provisions of the Warwick injunction, in addition to forbidding a reoccupation of the Registry, restrained the defendants 'by themselves, their servants or agents or otherwise' from removing, copying or in any way publishing, or even disclosing the contents or making any use of, documents from the Registry, or any other 'confidential documents the property of the plaintiffs'. This provision was used by the University authorities effectively to prevent quotation from or even reference to these documents by the national press, radio or television. Only the local press, and especially the *Birmingham Post*, upheld the journalist's tradition of publication without fear when the public interest so requires. So while events at the University received some publicity, the actual evidence which was the basis for the attack on the running of the University was little publicized nationally. Only on 26 February was the injunction against publication lifted, following internal pressure within the University, especially from staff.

How could the injunction have this effect? Of the twenty-one named defendants one, Sue Armstrong, was not any person known at the University; and while each of the other twenty had probably at some time been in the Registry, they were in no sense the ringleaders, and fewer than half had played any major role at all. The Vice-Chancellor stated in Assembly on

23 February that the names had been compiled 'in the emergency of the moment'; they seemed in fact to be students who
had in some way been prominent in the University in the past,
or were for some other reason known to the University officials
who observed the early stages of the sit-in. Following the service of the injunction, and after news of it had spread, a number of those named met to discuss the matter. Having taken
informal legal advice, they decided to dissociate themselves
immediately from the sit-in and return any documents that
may have been in their possession to the places where they had
been found. Probably all the documents taken from the
Registry had been removed well before the service of the injunction. Indeed the Montgomery letter and report, which had
been taken by E. P. Thompson, had been published by him to
all University staff on Thursday morning. Thus the injunction
was too late to prevent removal of documents. Could it prevent the discussion or publication by persons not party to the
injunction of documents that had been removed, and in many
cases had already received wide circulation?

The Montgomery correspondence had been freely available
in the University from Thursday 12 February, and on Monday 16 February the duplicated dossier containing a selection of documents found in the Registry had been widely distributed in the University (no students named in the injunction
had any hand in compiling or distributing this dossier). Many
of the documents from the Registry were therefore easily available to reporters. The *Birmingham Post* sought the advice of
its London solicitors and was told that only documents obtained from the named students after service of the injunction
were covered by it. Consequently on Saturday 14 February it
published extracts from the Montgomery correspondence; on
Tuesday 17 February extracts from the Wolf letter, the minute
of the Administration meeting on leafleting outside a Kenilworth school, and the Montgomery letter again; and finally
on 18 February it published extracts from correspondence between Automotive Products Ltd and the Vice-Chancellor about
a meeting addressed by a lecturer. These last were supplied to
the *Birmingham Post* by the lecturer concerned, who had been
shown them by students, and had read them out at the staff

meeting on Friday 13 February. The *Coventry Evening Telegraph* quoted the Montgomery letter on 14 February and the other correspondence mentioned above on 17 February.

The national press, however, were largely silent. The *Observer* gave some brief quotes from the Wolf correspondence on 15 February; others papers, such as the *Telegraph* and the *Express*, carried passing references to the documents (the latter, having contacted the headmaster of William Ellis School, took up that angle of the story). Even the major critique 'Warwick: The Business University' by E. P. Thompson in *New Society* on 19 February carried only extracts from the Montgomery letter. In particular *The Times* and *Sunday Times* had access to much of the material, and the editorial staffs of both papers were keen to publish extracts. Yet neither paper did so until after the injunction against publication had been lifted, and indeed in its 22 February edition the *Sunday Times* was reduced to a lame summary of the *New Society* piece.

A leader in *The Times* of 21 February (see p. 133) explained that this reticence was due to legal advice that: 'It is established law that such an injunction not only restrains those who are party to it but anyone who with knowledge of the injunction takes action which would have the effect of frustrating the injunction.' As the issuing of the injunction had been widely publicized, this interpretation of its effect would mean that almost anyone who had followed the events at Warwick, including most of the members of the University, would be in contempt of court if they even discussed the contents of any of the documents with anyone else. And yet, as *The Times* itself pointed out, 'no one who is not a party to an injunction can apply to have it removed or appeal against it, even though the effect of the injunction may be to restrain him from raising matters of great importance to himself'. As W. E. Hall commented in a signed article in the *Birmingham Post* on 27 February (aptly entitled 'This Shameful Silence'), the obvious conclusion to be drawn from that was: 'If they had no standing to appeal against the injunction, then manifestly they could not be bound by it. They could publish without being damned.'

The advice which the national newspapers were receiving seems to have been based on a bizarre case of 1897, Seaward *v.* Paterson. There a tenant had been enjoined from holding boxing matches on the leased premises, had ignored the injunction and had organized such a contest, with the help of some friends. The tenant and two others were committed for contempt, the appeal court holding after careful consideration that although the tenant's friends were not party to the injunction, 'a person who knowingly assists another who is restrained by an injunction is liable to committal for contempt ...'. But if the persons named in the injunction are not themselves breaking it, how can someone else be committed for aiding them?

The position would therefore seem to be that if the newspapers did not obtain their copies of documents from anyone named in the injunction, those named persons would not be publishing the documents, so there would be no breach of the injunction. The only disputable point would be how far the court would require newspapers to verify the source of their information. Given the serious, quasi-criminal nature of contempt proceedings, it seems unlikely that the court would require a newspaper to do more than ask its immediate contact the source of the documents. Even so, it is no doubt true that a newspaper with a good man on the spot (as the *Birmingham Post* had) was in a better position to satisfy itself about the source of its information than one which had the documents read to it by a stranger on the telephone.

Even in the event of a court holding that a newspaper was aiding a party to the injunction – for instance if it had obtained a document from such a party – the case for committal is not proved. There would for the first time be an opportunity to challenge the basis of the injunction, which was not possible at the original *ex parte* hearing. An injunction restraining publication of documents is based on a kind of property right in confidential information. Clearly a strong argument could be made that no such private rights exist in relation to documents whose publication is in the public interest. Indeed the courts have repeatedly made that very point: '... there is no confidence as to the disclosure of iniquity' (Gartside *v.* Outram, 1856); confidentiality does not extend to 'any misconduct of such a nature that it ought in the public interest to be disclosed to others' (Initial Services Ltd *v.* Putterill, 1967); 'there are some things which may be required to be disclosed in the public interest, in which event no confidence can be prayed in aid to keep them secret' (Fraser *v.* Evans, 1969).

Whatever view is taken of the implications of the various documents discovered in the Warwick files, none of those published can be said to relate to matters of purely private or personal concern. In fact, they clearly raised issues which merited thorough public discussion. It has been argued that the confidentiality of all information received by a body such as a University should be guaranteed, to ensure that correspondents could express themselves freely and without fear of embarrassment, even on matters of public concern. In fact, the conducting of public affairs in secret by those in authority can only reinforce the principle of power without responsibility.

If, therefore, the national press had displayed more of the crusading journalism demonstrated, on this occasion, by the *Birmingham Post*, they might well have found the law to be less inimical to publication in the public interest than their lawyers supposed.

However, the University was not slow to reinforce the reluctance of the communications media to ignore their over-cautious legal advisers. On Tuesday 17 February a spokesman for the University stated: 'A High Court injunction has been granted prohibiting the publication of documents removed by undergraduates from the administration and registry building.' At best this statement was gravely misleading, since it did not mention that the injunction applied only to twenty-one named students. This impression was not dispelled by the remainder of the statement:

Newspaper reports have appeared in the course of which the contents of certain documents to which these injunctions relate are disclosed. The University has been advised by their solicitors that any person who, even though not a party to the proceedings and not included in the injunctions, aids and abets a defendant in committing a breach of them, may himself be guilty of contempt of court and may be proceeded against accordingly.

Again, the unqualified association of publication and aiding and abetting is seriously misleading.

This statement was released through the Press Association wire at about 5.30 pm on Tuesday 17 February. The *Birmingham Post* ignored it and published the extracts from the documents on 18 February. *New Society* does not take a wire service and was unaware of the statement until about 6 pm on Wednesday, when Linklaters & Paines rang up the editor. By this time the copies of *New Society* containing the extracts had been printed. The editor was of the view that he was not covered by the injunction, a view which was reinforced by a telephone call to the *Birmingham Post*. No other national newspapers attempted to step out of line, but at York University the students' newspaper, *Nouse*, was planning to publish the documents. When the issue appeared, however, only blank spaces were to be found where the documents had been expected. The paper's printers had heard of the injunction and insisted that the students discover its scope. The students rang up the Warwick Administration and had dictated to them the statement of 17 February. Upon reading this the printer, in spite of appeals from the students, refused to print the documents.

The University Administration and its solicitors had also been busy on another front. On Thursday 19 February the solicitors wrote to the Press Council, not making any official complaint, but stating what had been published in the *Birmingham Post*, *Coventry Evening Telegraph* and *New Society*, in the hope 'that newspapers will be advised by the Press Council not to publish any further confidential information' (*Birmingham Post*, 24 February, quoting a University spokesman). In their letter to the Press Council the solicitors stated that the University had no intention of commencing legal proceedings against the journals named, partly 'in the light of Lord Radcliffe's forthcoming inquiry' and partly because 'the newspapers concerned appear to have believed that they were entitled to publish the documents....' The reasoning is at once cryptic and opaque, but the statements betray a lack of confidence in the Administration's legal and moral position. Not surprisingly, the reply by the Secretary of the Press Council was unsympathetic:

I have noted your remarks and your view of the legal situation, also the decision of your clients not to take action in respect of the publications mentioned.

The Press Council, however, does not in any circumstance supplement or supersede the processes of the law.

While I appreciate your object in bringing the matter to my attention I do not see how I can institute any action before the Press Council (*Birmingham Post*, 26 February).

However abortive in the result, between 19 February and 25 February this action of the University's gave it an additional lever for use against any national newspaper that was thinking of publishing the documents.

It can be seen, therefore, that rather than debate in public the serious issues raised by the discovery of the documents, the University authorities preferred to attempt by any means to suppress publication of the evidence that was the basis of its critics' case. In particular they succeeded in making a technically weak injunction have an effect far beyond its terms. At Manchester two weeks later an injunction was clumsily used by remote authorities against students whose mood had been gravely misjudged. The case of the Warwick documents shows that worried newspaper editors and cautious legal advisers are a better target for this unpredictable legal blunderbuss.

Chapter 6
Documents

Students and Staff
E. P. Thompson to all academic staff, 12 February 1970   124
Statement issued of motions passed at an informal
    meeting of staff on 13 February 1970   125
Senate statement, 14 February 1970   126
Proceedings of Union General Meeting, 16 February 1970   127
Notes for Professor Epstein's speech, 16 February 1970   128
Amended notice from Lord Radcliffe, 19 February 1970   130

Injunctions and the Press
The injunction   131
'The Equity of Injunctions', *The Times* third leader,
    21 February 1970   133
'The Right to Publish', *Birmingham Post* 'Comment',
    24 February 1970   134

The Tyzack Report   136

Hodgkinson to Butterworth, 18 January 1967   143

11 February 1970: Students Open Registry Files
12 February 1970: Registrar's Notice to All Staff

Registrar's notice to all staff

The University of Warwick
12 February 1970

Certain statements have been made and a letter has been circulated to colleagues by Mr E. P. Thompson suggesting that the University maintains records about the outside political activities of staff and students. The purpose of this note is to say quite categorically that this is not so. Inevitably members of the public write to the University from time to time about the outside activities of its members. When replies are sent to such letters, it is stated that the University has no concern with the political or off-campus activities of either staff or students.

D. W. Dykes
Registrar

The Montgomery Report

From Gilbert Hunt of Rootes Motors to the Vice-Chancellor

PO Box 441
Bowater House
Knightsbridge
London SW1

18 March 1969

J. B. Butterworth Esq., MA, JP
The University of Warwick
Coventry, Warwicks

Strictly confidential

My dear Jack

At my request, Mr N. P. Catchpole, our Director of Legal Affairs, attended a meeting of the Coventry Labour Party on 3 March, which was being addressed by Dr D. Montgomery.
    As you will see from the attached notes of the meeting,

nothing was said by him which would involve prosecution under the 1919 Aliens Restriction Act, but I felt it would be advisable nevertheless for you to have a copy of these notes for your confidential files.

Sincerely
Gilbert (signed)

Note: Bowater House is occupied by Rootes Motors. One of the directors is Gilbert A. Hunt; he is also a co-opted member of the University Council, and Chairman of its Building Committee.

Report by N. P. Catchpole, Legal Adviser of the Rootes Organization, of the meeting of the Coventry Labour Party on 3 March 1969

Accompanied by Mr T. Norton, Security Officer, Stoke, I duly attended a meeting of the Coventry Labour Party at its offices on the evening of Monday 3 March.

The guest speaker, Dr D. Montgomery, spoke for about half an hour to an audience of eight people including the chairman who, incidentally, is an ex-Labour Councillor by the name of Edwards. I think that one member of the audience may have been Mr Bob Mitchell, one of the left-wing students at Warwick University. The remainder included Mr H. Finch, whom I understand is a shop steward at Dunlops; with the exception of a shorthand writer who is on Norton's staff there were no other Rootes employees present.

Montgomery's speech was I felt poor in content. He warned the meeting of the danger of accepting measured day-work which he said would remove the negotiating powers of the local shop stewards and particularly when associated with automation was entirely contrary to the best interests of the workers. He did not however give any specific examples to justify this allegation but merely referred to the general experience in American industry.

After he had finished, three members of the audience, in-

cluding Mr Finch, paid markedly lukewarm tribute to the
speech. These three were strong supporters of the All Trades
Union Alliance. They felt that all members of the working
community should unite:

1. To bring down the Wilson government and organize a political alternative to fight the Conservatives at the next election.
2. That they should organize sympathy strikes to support the
Ford workers in their current dispute.
3. That ultimately the only answer was for the workers to seize
the factories.

Dr Montgomery was, I felt, particularly careful not to associate himself with any of these suggestions.

My personal conclusions based admittedly on a limited
knowledge of the local situation were as follows:

1. Nothing that Montgomery said could involve any question
of a prosecution under the Aliens Restriction Act.
2. Montgomery's speech revealed a very definite bias against
employers in general. I can only guess from seeing the man
that he would be most likely to exhibit a similar bias in his
lectures at the University. If this is the case the students would
most certainly be exposed to a most undesirable indoctrination,
as I do not think he would put the other point of view at all.
3. The three supporters of the All Trades Union Alliance are
dedicated subversives. I am doubtful if they [are sufficiently
intelligent to] * carry much weight with their fellow employees,
by whom they would be regarded, I would have thought, as
mere 'hotheads'.

N. P. Catchpole

* These words are erased in the original.

Who is Dr Hyman?

From the Deputy Managing Director of Automotive Products Ltd to the Vice-Chancellor

Automotive Products Ltd
Leamington Spa
Tel: 2700
Director's Office

5 February 1969

J. B. Butterworth Esq., MA, JP
University of Warwick
Coventry

Private and confidential

Dear Vice-Chancellor

Further to our conversation, I enclose the documents referred to. The only additional information I can give is:

1. The smaller document was distributed outside our works on 31 January by people that we believe to be students of the University.
2. We sent a representative to the meeting on 3 February, at Coundon Road, which was attended by only twenty-eight people.
3. The longer document was distributed at that meeting, and Dr Hyman's talk was very much in line with its contents.
4. We are not proposing to send anyone to the next meeting because we do not wish to draw attention to our interest in what is going on.

I will, of course, let you know of any further developments that we hear about.

Kind regards
Yours sincerely
S. M. Parker
Deputy Managing Director

An unsigned carbon of a letter from the University to the Deputy Managing Director of Automotive Products Ltd

6 February 1969

S. M. Parker Esq.
Deputy Managing Director
Automotive Products Ltd
Leamington Spa
Warwicks

Private and confidential

Thank you very much for your letter and contents. I am very sorry that it should have happened, but as you know we have no more control over what our people do in their spare time than you have. I shall be grateful, however, if there are any further developments to know about them.

From Gilbert Hunt to the Vice-Chancellor

P.O. Box 441
Bowater House
Knightsbridge
London SW1

7 February 1969

J. B. Butterworth Esq.
110 Kenilworth Road
Coventry
Warwicks

Dear Jack

Attached is a photostat of a leaflet being handed out at our factory gates by some Warwick University students.

I am sending this to your house as I don't think it ought to go to the University.

Who, by the way, is Dr Richard Hyman?

Sincerely
Gilbert (signed)

Reject This Man

From the Headmaster of William Ellis School to the Tutor for Admissions, Faculty of Science

William Ellis School
Highgate Road
London NW5

17 February 1969

The Tutor for Admissions
Faculty of Science
University of Warwick
Coventry

Strictly confidential

Dear Sir

Michael Wolf, Course No. 37220, Molecular Science

I write to you concerning the application for entry in 1969 of M. Wolf of this school. I find it necessary to add to the comments made on the UCCA entry form concerning his preoccupation with student politics. He is now a committee member of the London Schools Action Group, engaged in the organizing of protests and demonstrations concerning school government, etc. His name appeared in *The Times Educational Supplement* of 10 January, expressing his intention to embark on militant action when necessary.

I felt it was important that you should be aware of this in making your decision. I would prefer this communication to be treated very confidentially, and should be pleased to receive your comments.

Yours faithfully
Sydney L. Baxter (signed)
Headmaster

(Written at foot of letter: **Reject This Man, J.B.B.** (signed).)

From the Registrar to the Headmaster of William Ellis School

4 March 1969

S. L. Baxter, MA
Headmaster
William Ellis School
Highgate Road
London NW5

Personal

Dear Headmaster

I am writing to acknowledge your letter of 17 February, addressed to the Tutor for Admissions, regarding Michael Wolf. The Vice-Chancellor has asked me to say how very much obliged we were to you for writing in this way. We really are most grateful to you.

You may wish to know – privately – that the course selector has decided not to make an offer in this case. But it will no doubt be a week or two before the candidate hears of this officially through UCCA.

Yours sincerely
Registrar

A Disturbing State of Affairs

Sometime during the last week of November 1969, at the request of two school pupils, three students (short-haired males) from the University of Warwick stood outside the Abbey High School for Girls, Kenilworth, and distributed leaflets concerning a meeting of the Coventry Schools Action Union to be held at 42 High Street, Kenilworth, the home of three other University students (two female and one male).

After the leaflets had been distributed and the meeting had been held, the Warwick students left the Schools Action Union to its own devices and thought no more about the subject.

They were thus somewhat surprised to find evidence, during the occupation of the Registry, that their mild involvement in actions which were by no means illegal had caused a flurry of activity in upper echelons of the Establishment, the intent of which had been to pressurize the University into controlling these extra-campus activities of its students.

How the confusion between the two separate groups of students arose is not clear.

The sequence of letters that follows, at first glance possibly rather trivial, points to some disturbing implications, which are discussed in the editor's 'Personal Comment' (p. 146).

From the Education Officer of Warwickshire to the Vice-Chancellor

C. J. Chenevix-Trench, MBE, MA
County Education Officer
Warwickshire County Council
County Education Office
22 Northgate Street
Warwick

1 December 1969

Personal

J. B. Butterworth Esq., MA, JP
Vice-Chancellor
University of Warwick
Coventry

Dear Mr Butterworth

I enclose a copy of the paper handed out recently by the three students of the University to pupils coming out of the Abbey High School, Kenilworth. It was dictated to my secretary over the telephone today by Mr Forsyth, and Mr Douty asked me to send it to you.

Yours sincerely
C. J. Chenevix-Trench (signed)

Note: Alderman Douty is Chairman of the Warwickshire County Council Education Committee and a member of the University Council.

Is Your School Democratic?

Are you allowed to express your views?

Is your future life dependent on the whims of your headmaster and staff (the headmaster must give a report and reference for university, college and first job).

Are school games, especially rugby, compulsory? Rugby football is often played just to keep up the school's reputation.

IS THE CANE USED IN YOUR SCHOOL?

Such punishment should be outlawed. It is a barbaric remnant of the brutality of the last century. Only in a few countries in the world are teachers allowed to use it.

ARE YOU VICTIMIZED FOR UNORTHODOX APPEARANCES?

Has your school petty rules about such things as length of hair, length of skirts and coats, the wearing of rings and nail varnish, make-up, style of shoes, the colour of socks, and other trivial matters completely unrelated to education?

ARE YOUR SCHOOL SOCIETIES' NOTICES, PUBLICATIONS AND VIEWS CENSORED?

Must school societies have official approval from the headmaster? Are you allowed to put up notices, posters, even ones connected with school activities, without permission? Does the headmaster censor all material going into the school magazine, the end result being a stereotyped publication?

Above all, are you allowed to express your thoughts without risking punishment?

WHY IS EDUCATIONAL EXPENDITURE SO LOW?

Why are qualified teachers after years of training only paid £18 a week? Why do so many classes have over forty pupils? Why are education cuts being made left, right and centre?

We support the teachers' strike.

All over the country Schools Action Union groups are being set up. These are groups of school students who are interested in pressing for a better, more democratic education.

If you would like to discuss the nature of your education or possibly form a Kenilworth Schools Action Union, come to a meeting at 7.30 pm on Tuesday 2 December at 42 High Street, Kenilworth. *Published by the Coventry Schools Action Union.*

An unsigned letter from the University to Alderman H. H. C. Douty, Chairman of the Warwickshire Education Committee

2 December 1969

Alderman H. H. C. Douty
Northend
Dunchurch
Nr Rugby

Thank you very much for letting me know so quickly about the distribution of a pamphlet outside the Abbey High School in Kenilworth. I received this morning a copy of the paper which was being handed out. Of the three persons you mention, Judith Condon and Ann Freud are members of the University. I have turned up their records this morning and you may be interested to know that in each case the headmistress of the girl gave her an absolutely first-class reference. We have no recollection of the third, Julian Harber, having any connexion with the University. I am very distressed that this should have happened and have already spoken to the headmaster. If there are any further instances I hope I shall be informed.

As you may know, universities have no authority over students outside the University. By law they are adult at the age of eighteen and will shortly receive the vote. As I said on the telephone, a Vice-Chancellor has now by law no further influence over the outside activities of his students than the Managing Director of Rootes has over the outside activities of his employees. However, I greatly sympathize with the headmaster. I would like to be kept informed and if I can see an opportunity for taking action you may be sure I will do so.

I notice that the paper which was distributed is alleged to be published by the Coventry SAU. Do you think it would be worthwhile making inquiries in Coventry? There may be more behind this than the action of a few students.

Note: Early in December a constituent of Dudley Smith, M P, wrote to Enoch Powell, M P, drawing attention to the leaflet. Enoch Powell wrote to Dudley Smith, who in turn wrote to R. M. Willis, Clerk to the County Council, commenting that the letter, on the face of it, revealed a disturbing state of affairs. The story at Warwick resumes early in January 1970.

From the Warwickshire Education Officer to the Registrar

C. J. Chenevix-Trench, MBE, MA
County Education Officer
Warwickshire County Council
Education Office
22 Northgate Street
Warwick
2 January 1970

D. W. Dykes Esq., MA
The Registrar
The University of Warwick
Coventry

Personal

Dear Mr Dykes

I enclose for your *confidential* information a copy of the correspondence with Mr Dudley Smith, M P, which we discussed today on the telephone, and a copy of my reply to the Clerk of the County Council.

Yours sincerely
C. J. Chenevix-Trench (signed)

From the Warwickshire Education Officer to the Clerk of Warwickshire County Council

C. J. Chenevix-Trench, MBE, MA
County Education Officer
Warwickshire County Council
Education Office
22 Northgate Street
Warwick

2 January 1970

R. M. Willis
Clerk to the Council

Dear Sir

Kenilworth Castle High School
Distribution of Leaflet

In reference to your letter of 29 December, the following information will, I hope, enable you to reply to Mr Dudley Smith, M P.

Councillor Forsyth (Kenilworth Second) drew Alderman Douty's attention to this incident soon after it happened. He was able to give Mr Douty the names of the three students who were distributing the leaflets, two of whom were undergraduates of the University of Warwick. The students were, according to Mr Forsyth, not on the school premises, but just outside the gates on the public highway, when they handed out the leaflet.

Mr Douty spoke to the Vice-Chancellor by telephone, and protested at the students' action. The Vice-Chancellor expressed great concern at the incident, since although the students appeared not to be in breach of the law or the University's regulations, they were clearly damaging the good name of the University. He promised to consider what action he could take.

The Vice-Chancellor is now in India, and it is not possible to ascertain what, if anything, he has felt able to do. It is quite clear, however, that the University authorities are placed in a difficult position if, as it seems, the students have not placed themselves within the reach of formal disciplinary measures. A false step could easily make matters worse.

I think myself that it must be left to the Vice-Chancellor's judgement what, if anything, can be done about this particular case. It has been made abundantly clear that he is much concerned and not disposed to dismiss it lightly, for obvious reasons.

I would suggest, therefore, that Mr Dudley Smith might be informed that the Chairman of the Education Committee took the matter up personally with the Vice-Chancellor at the time, and was satisfied that the University authorities took a serious view of the incident and would consider how best to deal with it. There has, so far as we know, been no similar incident since then, involving students of the University. If there had been we would certainly have heard of it.

I would be grateful for a copy of your reply to Mr Dudley Smith.

Yours sincerely
C. J. Chenevix-Trench (signed)

Extracts from the minutes of weekly meetings of Officers of Council (no date)

In the course of the meeting the Vice-Chancellor received a telephone call from Alderman Douty complaining that three girls had distributed leaflets outside the Kenilworth Abbey High School, calling a meeting of a 'Schools Action Group'. The girls, who were thought to be University of Warwick students, were named as Judith Condon, Ann Frued [sic] and Julianne [sic] Harber of 42 High Street, Kenilworth. It appeared that an angry parent had telephoned Mr Forsyth, who was Chairman of the Governors of the Kenilworth Abbey High School. The Vice-Chancellor pointed out that Mr Forsyth had defended the University when the question of the County Council grant was discussed, and he was anxious that the name of the University should not be brought into disrepute and the goodwill of the County Council lost. Alderman

Douty, it was clear, expected some action to be taken. The problem of taking action over an incident outside the University, and not in contravention of University regulations, was discussed. It was thought that the Vice-Chancellor might speak to Poulton about the incident, and possibly have a word with Mr Forsyth. ...

The Registrar reported on the news from Essex about Julian Harber, the third person, presumably, to have distributed leaflets outside Kenilworth High School in December; it raised the question of whether he was qualified to take a higher degree at Warwick. It was suggested that candidates from Essex might be carefully screened in future. The VC asked for a note on the whole Kenilworth incident. The AVC to talk to police about 42 High Street, Kenilworth.

The Growing Student Menaces
From one Vice-Chancellor to another ...

13 June 1967

Personal

I wonder whether you saw this section of *The Times Educational Supplement* on Friday. Is it not time that the universities went into action on this matter? What worries me is politicians and others campaigning for student rights *in universities* when, if what they say is correct, their arguments would apply equally well to colleges of education and technical colleges. I am afraid of a situation in a few years' time in which the colleges of education and technical colleges retain control over their students, but because of pressure we shall give way more and more to student organizations, and the kind of behaviour which recently occurred at LSE will be commonplace throughout universities in the land. Why is it that politicians and others are always asking for student concessions in the universities, and yet are silent about colleges of education and technical colleges where, in my limited experience, students are far less implicated in the government of their institutions.

Again in my limited experience, there are a number of industrialists who are openly saying that they would prefer the products of technical colleges to those of universities because the students coming from technical colleges have a greater sense of discipline and capacity for loyalty.

... and the reply

15 June 1967

Thank you very much for your letter and for the quotation from *The Times Educational Supplement* which I had seen. I would like to talk to you about this question. I devoted my Court speech this year with all the vigour I could to the question of the criticism of universities as ivory towers, but these things only get a limited circulation. I am sure you are right and that we ought to do something about the growing student menaces, though I must say I am groping as to how best to meet the situation. Perhaps we could carve out ten minutes at our next meeting.

Yours ever
(signed)

An unsigned carbon of a letter from the University to Professor Max Beloff, Fellow of All Souls College, Oxford

8 July 1968

Professor Max Beloff
All Souls College
Oxford

I am very sorry that I have to go to America for three days and that we shall not be meeting until November.

In the meantime, thank you very much for sending me a copy of your homily on universities and vice-chancellors. The real problem, at any rate in modern universities, is that vice-chancellors have responsibility without authority. Under the statutes and charters, the decisions are taken by Senate and Council, and the vice-chancellor who wants to be tough will never get the support that he needs. Under the statutes of Warwick, and I expect ours are much the same as other universities, Senate is required to regulate matters of discipline. No student can be expelled except by a vote of Senate. It is therefore almost impossible for a vice-chancellor to act on his own, because he will almost always be repudiated by the Senate, for in the discussion of those matters by Senates, inevitably the liberal-minded prevail because the academic is always reluctant to act in a crises [sic].

I very much agree with what you say and would add only one rider that in most of the universities where serious trouble has occurred at the moment of crises [sic] the real difficulty is not the students but the staff who assist, advise, and indeed sometimes direct the activities of the extreme student group.

We are taking legal advice about tenure of staff under the University statutes. In most universities a member can only be dismissed for 'good cause', which is tightly defined. Moreover, even if conduct of a member of staff can be deemed 'good cause' removal must secure in Council a majority of not less than two-thirds of those present and voting. On most councils, the laymen tend to be less regular attenders than the academics and, in practice, I suspect it will be difficult in any particular instance to get the necessary two-thirds majority. However, let us talk about the whole problem in September, for by then we should have had the benefit of Council's [Counsel's?] opinion.

An Inquiry about Reciprocal Arrangements
From a businessman to the Vice-Chancellor

16 September 1964

J. B. Butterworth Esq., MA, JP
University of Warwick
Coventry

Dear Mr Butterworth

My family have old business connexions in your area and I have seen the University's announcement in the August issue of *The Director*. I would be pleased to receive further details of your appeal and to know what, if any, reciprocal arrangements can be offered to the sons or daughters of directors or employees whose firms contribute to the welfare of the University; the establishment of which has brought great pleasure to the district.

For example, I have a [child] who has just passed [four subjects] in grades two or three, [one] in four and [one] in six. Would [it] have any prospect of entering the University if [it] took any, and if so what, A-levels? And one of my co-directors has a son three or four years younger, who would probably be interested in sending him to our new University.

I shall be interested to hear from you further.

Yours sincerely
(signed)

Note: Name and address withheld. The correspondent's child was admitted to the University. There is no evidence whatever that this admittance was in any way improper. This letter is included because it illustrates dramatically the kind of attitude to a university that one businessman seems to consider reasonable and natural.

Long-Haired Louts

From a Foundation to the Vice-Chancellor

3 December 1968

J. B. Butterworth, MA, JP
The University of Warwick
Coventry
Warwicks

Dear Vice-Chancellor

Thank you very much indeed for sparing me so much of your time when I visited the University yesterday, and thank you again for the most enjoyable lunch.

I was very interested to see round this wonderful new University and how glad I was to see the fruits of British workmanship in such excellent buildings.

However, I cannot say that I was impressed by your students; how sad it is to see these long-haired louts wearing jeans and sandals flopping around in such splendid surroundings. What a pity you cannot order them to wear some sort of uniform – if only a cap and gown.

I look forward to hearing from you, in due course, with your approach to the foundation for funds towards your new auditorium – at least I think this is what we decided it should be called.

Yours sincerely
(signed)

An unsigned carbon of a letter from the University to R. J. Kerr-Muir, Treasurer of the University and a Director of Courtaulds, concerning this letter, contained the following comment:

I agree very much with him (except for caps and gowns) and thought you should see the view of someone who was visiting the University for the first time, first the approval of the architecture, and I grow tired of the denegation [sic] of the architect by staff and students alike, and second his views about students. I still think we are giving too much away to them, not only in Warwick but in universities generally.

Students and Staff

From E. P. Thompson to all academic staff

Centre for the Study of Social History
University of Warwick

12 February 70

To all academic staff

Dear Colleague

At about 8.30 pm last night I was rung by a student in the Registry, who informed me that an important document had come to light in a file in an unlocked office which related to my former colleague in the Centre for the Study of Social History, Professor David Montgomery of the University of Pittsburgh.

You will recall that David Montgomery was seconded to us for two years (1967–9) as Senior Lecturer in the History of American Labour, through the kind offices of the American Council of Learned Societies, which provided the funds for initiating this new field of study at Warwick University.

Without making any judgement as to the propriety of inspecting files, I felt it necessary to go to the Registry and inspect the document.

I was shown two documents which – having read – I abstracted from the file. I now hold them, and will, if required, place them in the custody of the Association of University Teachers. The documents are fully copied and attached to this letter.

The following comments may be made:

Professor Montgomery is a scholar of distinction and, in inviting him to take up this post, the University took the advice of eminent academic advisers in the United States. He accepted a cut in both salary and status to come here, worked at the fullest stretch while here – playing an active part both in the Centre and in the School of History – serving on the Board of Arts and on several University committees – advising the library on purchases, and initiating the successful MA course in Comparative Labour History. As an expert in labour movements he was also invited to attend or to address several meetings of trade unions and Labour Party bodies.

What might surprise the Coventry City Labour Party and the Coventry Trades Council is that our Vice-Chancellor has been in receipt of private reports of such events. If the implication of these documents is that some person was meditating deportation proceedings against Dr Montgomery, then I have little doubt that you will be as astonished as I am.

I am suggesting to the Secretary of the AUT that he might wish to call an early meeting to discuss the further implications of this matter.

Yours sincerely
E. P. Thompson

Statement issued of motions passed at an informal meeting of staff on 13 February 1970

1. This meeting deplores the keeping of political documents on staff and students and demands the immediate destruction of any such documents now in existence.

This meeting further demands a solemn pledge that on receipt of such information in future from outside the University it should be sent to the member of the University concerned and further that the University should inform the senders of the information of its actions and say that it will not be interested in receiving such information again.

2. This meeting nevertheless extends its goodwill to all parties involved in the current disturbance and retains an open mind on the issues involved until a proper inquiry can be instituted.

It also expresses its willingness to cooperate in any constructive attempt to develop and strengthen the University.

Statement regarding recent events issued by the Senate following its meeting of 14 February 1970

Senate condemns the disruption of the work of the University, the physical damage, the breaking open of confidential files and the intimidation of administrative staff which occurred at the recent sit-in.

As a first priority, in order to restore the normal working order of the University, an injunction has been sought and obtained against a number of named individuals.

Charges will be made against persons who appear to have gone beyond the bounds of tolerable behaviour and to have committed grave disciplinary offences. (Charges against students are heard by a Discipline Committee of five members, two of whom are students. The procedure gives full opportunity to those concerned to defend themselves and be represented, and to appeal against the decisions of the committee.)

Senate is concerned that there is disquiet about the retention of information received by the University about the political activities of members of staff and students, and has unanimously asked the Chairman of Council to invite the Chancellor, the Viscount Radcliffe, to inquire into the procedures followed with regard to such information. The Chancellor has agreed to hold the inquiry as a matter of urgency.

Senate has set up a committee to consider the methods by which guarantees can be given that no improper use is made of political information received by the University, and that in particular unsolicited information of this kind can be disclosed to the person concerned.

Senate fully realizes the importance of adequate social buildings to the life of everyone in the University. It welcomes the Council's recent decisions as the basis for the planning of social buildings and hopes that the detailed plans and a settlement of policy for administration, which are tasks requiring the co-operation of staff and students, will go forward with all due speed.

Senate is treating as a matter of urgency the need to achieve a radical improvement in cooperation and understanding within the University.

D. W. Dykes
Registrar

Proceedings of Union General Meeting, 16 February 1970

Copy of telegram sent to Mr David Montgomery

We, the largest meeting ever held of the students and staff of the University of Warwick, extend to you our apology for the contemptible evidence that has come to light as to private reports being discovered in the University files upon your political activities and opinions. We assure you that we knew nothing of this matter, utterly deplore it, and will do all we can to ensure that such incidents will not recur.

Motions passed

1. This meeting regrets any distress, fear or anxiety which may have inadvertently been caused to the clerical staff during the occupation of the Registry. But reiterates its demands that no disciplinary action or legal charges be brought.
2. This meeting:
a. Rejects the statement of the recent meeting of Senate (14 February 1970).
b. Denies the moral right of the present University Administration to bring any charges whatsoever against staff and students involved in recent events.
c. Expresses the urgent demand for a public inquiry into recent events and the administration of the University, to be conducted by an authority completely independent of the University and its connexions.
d. Supports the demand for an integrated social building under staff/student control.
3. This meeting of staff and students calls for a public inquiry into:
a. The structure, government and finance of the University, including the exercise by the Vice-Chancellor of his administrative powers.

b. All the allegations of improper conduct of members of the University Council.

c. The until now uninvestigated resignation of the last Registrar and two of his senior assistants.

d. The character and source of information as to the extra-academic activities of members of the University which are believed to be held in University files.

4. This meeting proposes that the students of the University intend to start a peaceful and orderly nationwide campaign to persuade the Privy Council to allow the majority membership of the University Council to consist of democratically elected staff and student representatives, and that the lay membership of the Council should represent the whole community.

It further proposes that the Senate and Vice-Chancellor should declare that they would be in sympathy with the aims of such a campaign.

5. In the light of recent events and with respect to the possibility of prosecution of certain members of the Union within two weeks, this meeting demands that the proposed Union Legal Aid Fund be set up immediately.

There were at least *850 staff and students* present and voting at this meeting.

Notes for a speech by Professor D. B. A. Epstein on 16 February 1970 at a meeting of students and staff of the University of Warwick

Members of the University

The sit-in and its consequences have had the effect of removing a tremendous amount of restraint on what I feel free to say. Chairmen of Departments are inevitably inhibited in saying what they really feel. It is only under conditions of publicity such as these we have at the moment that one can feel safe from retaliation. Even so my colleagues can confirm that I have only decided to make this speech with a considerable degree of trepidation.

Let us go back to 15 November 1963, when the draft charter and statutes were agreed by the Vice-Chancellor and nine of the original professors. These had been circulated to the professors only two days earlier. They were agreed with only minor amendments. The statutes give the Vice-Chancellor the power to refuse to admit any person as a student of the University without assigning any reason. At the Senate meeting on Saturday the Vice-Chancellor stated that he could remember exercising this power on only two or three occasions. I find unacceptable the exercise of this power on any occasion.

Let us now consider the origins of the sit-in – that is, the University's policy on social buildings. As far back as November 1967 a Union General Meeting voted unanimously in favour of a Union Building. On 7 November 1967 the University Council discussed the Union Building issue and on 5 December 1967 the Council reached the first of its final decisions on this question. The decision of Council was against having a building under Union control. Council thus consciously and deliberately flouted the Assembly, which it knew would be having an emergency meeting six days later. At that meeting of Assembly there were seventy-one votes in favour of a building under student control and thirteen against. On 6 February 1968 the Council insulted Assembly with the following minute:

That any opinion expressed by Assembly could not constrain Council in any way, but that such opinions might carry more weight if it was clear that all facets of any case had been fully considered.

On 19 February 1968 the Policy and Development Committee of Council set up a Working Party on Social Structure. By coincidence almost all the members of this Working Party had declared their opposition to a Union Building.

The Working Party met sixteen times and reported to Senate on 12 June 1968. At the Senate meeting four alternative proposals were voted on by a series of votes. In an attempt to ensure that the academic view would prevail, it had been previously agreed by members of Senate that the final vote would be *nem. con.* At the end of a series of votes Senate decided by thirteen votes to none in favour of a Union Building under student control. This was a vital meeting and the minutes of the meeting were vital. On 26 June 1968 Senate corrected a serious error in the minutes. However, on the day before, Council had met and taken its second final decision against a Union Building, using the incorrect minutes as a basis for its decision.

Well, the whole business goes on and on, so I won't go into the excruciating detail. A number of points can however be made:

1. In my view Council has usurped the power of Senate in this matter. The relevant statute says that Council should 'provide and maintain the buildings'. This statute has been, let us say, broadly interpreted. By what right do lay members of Council tell us how to allocate space between students and staff in a social building?

2. After more than two years of equivocation, evasion and error by the Council and the Vice-Chancellor, student opinion was understandably restive. I now feel most unhappy and indeed resentful that Senate, which has in the past had a reasonably good line on the Union Building issue, has been brought into confrontation with the students. Let the responsibility lie with those who created the situation.

For the above reasons I support the demand for an independent inquiry into the management of this University. If we have such an inquiry I would be glad to produce a number of examples from my confidential files of what I regard as serious abuses in the running of this University.

Amended notice from Lord Radcliffe

19 February 1970

I have been invited by the Chairman of the Council of the University to inquire into the procedures that have been followed in the University with regard to receiving and retaining information about political activities of the staff and of students. I have also been requested to take within the scope of my inquiry any allegations brought to me of improper administrative conduct within the University. The invitation has been made at the unanimous request of the Senate, and, as it is obvious that the question of these procedures is regarded as one of urgent importance, I have promised to undertake the inquiry.

To carry this out I have to inform myself of certain matters; briefly, in what ways such information comes into the possession of the University, what is done with it when received, and what, if any, use of it is made for any purpose of the University.

Much of this I can find out from University officials. But, in view of the disquiet that has arisen on this subject, I shall not be content unless I know that every person in the University who feels that he has any information or comments to contribute or any matter to complain of has had an opportunity of getting in touch with me direct and putting any relevant material before me.

I think that it will be most convenient for everyone if I nominate some place outside the University itself where such complaints or information can be lodged, together with any supporting evidence. I have accordingly asked Mr John Penn, of the firm of Messrs Rotherham & Co., Solicitors, of 8 The Quadrant, Coventry, to act as my secretary for this purpose. I shall be obliged if anyone wishing to communicate with me will do so through Mr John Penn at that address.

Radcliffe

Injunctions and the Press

The injunction

In the High Court of Justice
Queen's Bench Division   1970 T No. 840

Between the University of Warwick *Plaintiffs*
and
[21 names] *Defendants*

Upon hearing Counsel for the Plaintiffs *ex parte* it is ordered that the Defendants [21 names] and each of them:

1. By 9.00 am on Friday 13 February 1970, or within thirty minutes after service of this order whichever is the later, do give up occupation of and leave the building known as the Administration Building and Registry in the University of Warwick.

2. Be restrained until further order by themselves, their servants or agents or otherwise from re-entering the said Administration Building and Registry save for such purposes as the Plaintiffs permit them in accordance with the statutes and usages of the University so to do.

3. Be restrained until further order by themselves, their servants or agents or otherwise from entering upon or occupying or otherwise using any part of the buildings or premises of the Plaintiffs save for such purposes as they are permitted by the statutes and usages of the University so to do.

4. Be restrained until further order by themselves, their servants or agents or otherwise from further damaging any part of the Plaintiffs' buildings or premises or any property of the Plaintiffs thereon, or otherwise harming the same.

5. By 9.00 am Friday 13 February 1970, or within thirty minutes of the service of this order whichever is the later, deliver to the Plaintiffs all such books, papers or documents of whatsoever kind as the defendants have removed from the Administration Building and Registry in the University of Warwick, including all copies of any such documents, and be restrained by themselves, their servants or agents or otherwise from removing or copying any further such documents.

6. Forthwith be restrained by themselves, their servants or agents or otherwise from publishing or otherwise in any way disclosing the contents of or making any use of any documents removed by the defendants from the Administration Building or Registry in the University of Warwick, or any copies of any such documents, or of any other confidential documents the property of the Plaintiffs.

Notice

If you, the within-named Defendants, neglect to obey all or any of the orders recited in paragraphs 1 or 5 of this order, or if you disobey all or any of the orders recited in paragraphs 2, 3, 4 and

6 of this order, you will be liable to process of execution for the purpose of compelling you to obey the same.

[In handwriting] Leave to Plaintiffs to serve this order, if necessary, by substituted service either by communicating the words therein to the Defendants by loud-hailer or by leaving a copy of it in the Administration and Registry.

12.2.70

The Times third leader, 21 February 1970

The Equity of Injunctions

An important question of law has arisen in the case of the Warwick University injunctions. In the course of a student sit-in various confidential documents belonging to the University were taken. The University was granted an *ex parte* injunction to prevent any use being made of these documents by the students who had removed them. It is established law that such an injunction not only restrains those who are party to it but anyone who with knowledge of the injunction takes action which would have the effect of frustrating the injunction.

In this case a student at Sussex University who was in no way involved in the sit-in at Warwick appears to have been referred to in one of the documents. The gist of the matter is that his headmaster, in a confidential letter, told Warwick University about this student's connexion with the London Schools Action Group and, as a result of that, Warwick University decided not to admit him as a student.

This student naturally feels that an injustice was done to him and that his political activities should not have been made the subject of a report to a University where he was seeking entrance. This is obviously a perfectly reasonable complaint on his part. Some will feel that the headmaster exercised his discretion legitimately and others that he did not, but no one can maintain that the student in question is not an interested party. It is perhaps no damage to end up at Sussex University rather that at Warwick, but it is fortuitous that he received no lasting damage. In fact Sussex had been his first choice.

What is really disturbing is that the legal advice given to

The Times is that no one who is not a party to an injunction can apply to have it removed or appeal against it, even though the effect of the injunction may be to restrain him from raising matters of great importance to himself. This seems on the face of it to be unjust; a doctrine that anyone who is inhibited from action by an injunction is nevertheless not a party to that injunction seems in itself inherently inequitable. Apart from the injustice that may or may not have been done to the young man in question, a very important point in law has been raised.

Birmingham Post 'Comment', 24 February 1970

The Right to Publish

Until the weekend the affair of the confidential files at Warwick University involved simply how the University chose to deal with information it received about the activities of staff and students – an important enough issue in all conscience.

Since then the University has contrived, by its misconceived reference of the issue to the Press Council, to bring into question another issue of major public importance – the right to publish.

Nearly a fortnight ago students occupied the Registry at the University and found various confidential documents in the files. One, said to have been written by the Secretary of Rootes Motors, related to an American professor and suggested that his students might be exposed to 'a most undesirable indoctrination'. There were other documents too. They seem to us to raise a central issue of public importance. Precisely for this reason we decided to publish them, even though we deplored the way in which they had been revealed.

The University obtained an injunction against a number of named students preventing them from publishing the documents. It did not apply to us; and we have not been in touch with any of the named students. The documents, indeed, have been quite widely circulated.

The University has now written to the Press Council setting out what has happened and naming the *Birmingham Post*, the *Coventry Evening Telegraph* and *New Society*. A spokesman said no complaint had been made. 'We hope that newspapers will be advised by the Press Council not to publish any further confidential information,' he said.

This displays a misunderstanding of the Press Council's function. It considers complaints about the Press, or about the conduct of persons and organizations towards the Press. It does not advise newspapers on how to act in particular circumstances. It would get short shrift from the *Birmingham Post* – and most of the Press – if it tried.

But the University has done much worse than display an ignorance of procedure. It has had a remedy open to it ever since the first of our reports giving details of disturbing information revealed in the files. It could have sought an injunction to prevent any further publication by us. We should have fought the case vigorously, fortified by the comments of Lord Denning, Master of the Rolls, when the *Sunday Times* contested an attempt to prevent it publishing an article about a report made by a public relations consultant to the Greek government. Lord Denning said:

There are some spheres of activity in which the public concern is such that the newspapers, the Press and indeed everyone may be entitled to make it public – in the concern of all. The freedom of speech and expression is the foundation of that. If they are guilty of libel, or breach of confidence, or breach of copyright, that can be determined in the action hereafter, and the damages awarded against them.

The University has avoided this direct confrontation. It has not even made a complaint to us. Instead it has sought to silence the *Post* by indirect means, by recourse to a voluntary body like the Press Council with what is a complaint in effect, but not a complaint in name.

The University of Warwick would do well to stop this useless and unbecoming struggle to keep from the public what the public plainly has a right to know. The University must recognize that it is not a closed community. It must accept that the public may have a concern in how it runs its affairs. The disclosures have been disagreeable, and have been made disagreeably; but out of them, out of the inquiry being made by Lord Radcliffe, the Chancellor of the University, may come an understanding of what is involved in this complex issue of academic freedom. We have already said that the students stand in need of this. So, too, judging by its suppressive activities since the sit-in, does the University itself.

The Tyzack Report, 24 May 1968

Para. 24. Taken as a whole, the University is certainly inefficient by normal commercial or industrial standards; it is inefficient in its decision-making processes, in its administrative structure, and in many of its administrative practices. Some parts of the machine run with commendable smoothness and economy of effort, notably in the library and in the sections of the Registry dealing with routine procedures such as admissions, staff recruitment and internal examinations; but these areas are outbalanced by cumbersome and time-wasting procedures in parts of the Finance Office, very inefficient use of the excellent computer facilities offered by the City of Coventry, unduly lavish procedures in the parts of the Registry dealing with committee work, failures of communications and a good deal of inefficiency in the catering department, general lack of supervision and coordination in what might be termed the 'housekeeping' side of the University (which includes matters such as the administration of halls of residence, porters and cleaners), and undue absorption of the time and energy of many members of the academic staff in serving a ponderous and indecisive committee system. . . .

Para. 28. Finally, we come to a matter which lies on the fringe of our brief only, since it is largely concerned with imponderables and matters of judgement in the academic sphere. It seems difficult for us to ignore its existence, however, since it involves the expenditure of large sums of money. Roughly half the University's annual expenditure on income account is devoted to paying the salaries of the academic staff. It is difficult to envisage economies in this sphere which do not involve an increase in the ratio of students to academic staff, or an increase in the proportion of lower-paid senior staff.

Para. 29. Clearly only marginal changes in teaching costs can be expected, unless there is a countrywide change of view in universities, for no university alone could embark on revolutionary changes in academic structure. Nevertheless, marginal improvements are possible and should be actively sought at Warwick in the long-term interests of the University, which for many reasons demands expansion far beyond its present size. Such expansion will for the time being depend critically on the next quinquennial allocation of funds by the University Grants Committee, and there would be an obvious advantage if the University were able in present conditions of Treasury stringency to prove that its academic costs were competitive. Academics tend to be idealists, and they find any conflict between the ideal and the pragmatic correspondingly distasteful. In the long-term interests of the University, however, an unduly rigid attitude at the present time may well defeat its own objects; we suspect it might be wiser to bend a little before the financial wind and fight back later. ...

Para. 35. The appointment of a senior administrator of high calibre, who could provide the University of Warwick with the same degree of competence as would be found at key positions in a well-run business, appears to us to be the most important single step which the University could take towards putting its house in order. The need for such an appointment is making itself felt already in many ways.

Para. 36. The Vice-Chancellor's energies are at present quite clearly being dissipated by too deep an involvement in matters of day-to-day administration. Despite this involvement, however, our report as a whole shows how many administrative problems still remain to be solved. To say this is not intended in any sense to be read as a criticism of the Vice-Chancellor, but as a statement of the facts of his position.

Para. 37. The Vice-Chancellor has a vital role to play in maintaining the momentum and the quality of the University's growth and in nurturing its reputation for high academic achievement. He also has an external role which is no less important; he has to represent his University in the outside world, fostering its interests in the highest circles, attracting financial support, and enhancing its status by playing a part in the public life of the University world at large both inside and outside the United Kingdom. His image is its image. ...

Para. 41. It will be observed that our suggested terms of

reference for this appointment are designed to avoid giving the Administration any additional voting rights on academic committees. Unless Council so determines, moreover, the post of Deputy Vice-Chancellor would not carry security of tenure; the reasoning here is that this is primarily an administrative appointment, and we see no reason why it should not be treated by Council in the same way as a board of directors would treat the appointment of a General Manager. Alternatively, if security of tenure is to be offered (and this may become necessary in order to attract a suitable candidate), we recommend that this should not operate until the end of a two-year probationary period. It seems important to us that Council should be able to reconsider its appointment to the post of Deputy Vice-Chairman in the light of early experience, for the qualities required of the holder are not such as can be assessed with certainty at an interview, or even from his past experience. A man who has proved competent in many normal managerial situations might nevertheless fail in the special conditions of a university. Some unsuspected trait might prove politically divisive or personally antipathetic to academic staff to a degree calling for termination of the appointment while there was still time to avoid a disastrous commitment. . . .

Para. 44. We have mentioned already the title of a new post, tentatively called that of the Steward, which we think it essential to create at a senior level, directly answerable to the Deputy Vice-Chancellor. The Steward would take over from the Finance Officer the entire domestic administration of the University, comprising the 'hotel-keeping' functions (i.e. catering, the administrations of the halls of residence and social building) and a wide miscellaneous sector which includes such matters as porters, internal mail, transport services, cleaning, and printing and stationery.

Para. 45. The 'hotel-keeping' function will soon include a substantial business operation with an annual turnover well in excess of £100,000, namely that of accommodating vacation conferences and possibly tourist parties. The remaining miscellaneous sector of general administration is also becoming substantial, and will employ a greatly expanded staff if the proposal to run a cleaning service instead of employing contractors is accepted. It appears to have been an historical accident that either sector should have become a responsibility of the Finance Officer; he has not got the time to administer it effectively, nor is it appropriate that he should operate a system which he has the duty of controlling financially. . . .

Para. 73. It seems to us that at the University of Warwick, the committee system of government is in danger of running riot. We have been told that democracy has a special place in University life, and that there is constant political pressure from the rank and file of the academic staff claiming the right not only to be consulted more but to 'have a hand in decision-making'. The result in practice is already an amorphous and time-wasting system which has led to needlessly protracted argument, dilatoriness in the taking of decisions, uncertainty regarding the effective centres of power and action, and at times to conflicts of policy and incompatibility of decisions. The system, moreover, has shown itself to be capable of manipulation, partly because references to committees without executive powers can generally be relied on to devitalize unwelcome proposals or hold up action indefinitely.

Para. 74. Sooner or later, the University of Warwick will have to come to terms with the age-old conflict between democratic principles and effective government. In its early days, the policy of allowing everybody to have his say in nearly every cause and problem was workable. At its present size, the resulting system of committees and debating forums is a source of inefficiency. The system is fast running to seed as continuous play is given to the instinct to form a new committee for every new problem. The tendency, moreover, is to give such committees powers only to discuss, to consider, to advise, and even to consider the desirability of advising; all too often, they then report to an existing committee whose own terms of reference are themselves advisory only. We believe that the time has come when the University must not only call a halt to this process but actively set about the streamlining of its existing system.

Para. 75. One of the worst features of the present committee system results from the combination of an absence of effective delegation of powers, an absence of representational functions on higher committees, and overlapping committee membership. A battle lost by an individual on a working party can be renewed by him on the sponsoring committee itself, and renewed again in Senate or Council or both of them if the decision again goes against him. If he is tenacious, he may even succeed in getting a matter referred back down the line for further interminable argument, with the certainty that it will have to return by the same route before an effective decision can be taken.

Para. 76. It is not only time and incisiveness as such that is lost when a committee system proliferates. Time costs public money. Committees absorb not only the energies of salaried members of the academic staff whose primary function is supposed to be teaching and research, but also the time of the Registry staff who have to service the committees. Every time a committee talks and reports instead of taking action there are new committee papers to be written, new floods of stationery to members of superior committees (some members of which get the same paper a second time as members of the reporting committee), new demands on filing time and shelf space.

Para. 77. Significantly, and rather unexpectedly, a surprising number of senior but relatively disenfranchised members of the academic staff obviously accept the necessity that in certain controversial areas as well as matters of day-to-day detail the last word should lie with a small body having effective powers of decision. Even more significantly, however, this acceptance was qualified by the demand that they themselves should over the years have as good a chance as anyone else of serving their turn on the committees which matter. They were prepared to live with the suspicion, however justified or unjustified, that those on the most powerful bodies could influence decisions in favour of their own departments; but only if they had their own opportunity of redressing the balance in due course.

Para. 78. In practice, we believe that responsibility tends to come with powers of decision; it is in the committees' bearing no onus of action that irresponsibility flourishes. Our recommendations are tailored accordingly: a greater degree of delegation and more rotation are both recommended. We cannot emphasize too strongly, however, that whatever a committee's area of authority it has no power to seek implementation otherwise than through the Vice-Chancellor, unless the latter chooses to allow the committee to act directly on his behalf. . . .

Para. 116. There are a number of disturbing features in the situation. Of these, perhaps the most potentially dangerous one is the tendency towards a set of attitudes and practices similar to those found in negotiations between employers and trade unionists. The Student Liaison Committee has no powers and no positive, constructive functions. It is intended to be a forum for discussion, but there are strong pressures on both sides tending to make it an arena for confrontation. The Students' Council, like the executive committee of a trade union, discusses its grievances and comes forward with demands; the Vice-Chancellor's Committee, like the negotiating committee of an employers' association, concerts its own attitude and then faces the students with a solid front in the Liaison Committee. There seems to be in this system an open invitation to the development of a series of embattled positions.

Para. 117. This situation would be undesirable in any circumstances. It is doubly dangerous, however, in circumstances where students have genuine grievances as they have at the University of Warwick. If the seeds of conflict are there, and the machinery is such as to invite confrontation instead of cooperation, it will only be a matter of time before a genuine issue can be raised to red heat by extremist elements and then used as a pretext for demands which would not normally receive the backing of the preponderantly sensible mass of students.

Para. 118. One reason why we feel that the students have genuine grievances is that we had the opportunity of seeing some things through their eyes when we lived for three months in Rootes Hall. This not only meant that we shared their services and facilities but met them naturally in relaxed and social circumstances.

Para. 119. We informed the Vice-Chancellor of our own observations on some of the conditions in Rootes Hall, but more important than the detail is the fact that the students do have grievances. Many of these can no doubt be explained away, as, for example, the widespread conviction that the catering services are run at a profit by outside contractors. But the fact that grievances, whether real or imagined, exist is a cause for concern. Moreover, while objective grievances of this kind are a continual irritant it is our impression that there is a more fundamental grievance of a largely subjective nature.

Para. 120. Taking the academic staff as a whole, they seem to the students to be remote from and even indifferent to the student population. The tutor system is working well; but in general it seems to provide almost the only effective contact between the students and the staff apart from practical work in the laboratories and limited bridges being built by one or two members of staff in the student houses and halls of residence.

Para. 121. One member of the Registry staff has done a lot for the students, partly through his registry activities and partly because of his interest in team games. But most of the teaching staff disappear from the campus when lectures are over, leaving the scene to porters, barmen and students.

Para. 122. It can of course be claimed with some justice that teaching staff are not there to be nursemaids; they have their own wives and families to consider as well as students. If students have personal problems there is a good sprinkling of chaplains about the place, and they have a tutor. Their representatives can let off steam in the Liaison Committee. Unfortunately, however, the existence of a defence may have little impact on a grievance, partly because the defence may not be believed but more often because the owner of the grievance has not heard the explanation. What matters is that all too many students are indeed disgruntled, and feel a basic lack of interest on the part of the academic staff. Whatever, within reason, can be done to remedy this state of affairs should be put in hand before and not after an explosive situation has arisen. The University must somehow put across the message that the student is considered important as an adult member of the community, and that the authorities care about him and value him. ...

Para. 130. We recommend that the liaison function of the present Student Liaison Committee should in matters of detail and day-to-day working be undertaken by a small committee whose main function would be to provide a working link between the students and the Administration rather than the University at large.

Letter from G. E. Hodgkinson, Chairman of the Planning and Development Committee, to the Vice-Chancellor

1 Browett Road
Coventry

18 January 1967

Mr J. B. Butterworth, JP
Vice-Chancellor
University of Warwick
Coventry

Dear Jack

Few situations have shocked and hurt me more in nearly forty years of voluntary service in local government in this city than that relating to the proposal to make Kenilworth Road a *dual* carriageway. At meetings of the University and Coventry City Council Liaison Committee, strong opinion has been expressed about the threat to the form and character of the road innate in some of the proposals for development. Our fears about the violation of the road were apparently not unfounded, though we believed honestly that the dialogue between the officers of the County and City was going on in the hope of reaching an agreement on the technical aspects of the proposals *under discussion*. No account has been taken of the principles governing active and useful liaison, and the City Council is faced with an attempt to secure a *fait accompli*. . . .

You can imagine the feelings of members of the Coventry Council when faced with a scheme of road development which constitutes a threat to destroy the character and beauty of Kenilworth Road and to throw a spanner into the carefully considered work done in connexion with the Development Plan Review. In other words, to 'cock a snoot' and flout the opinion of the friends of the University in the City Council who have given unwavering support to almost everything you wanted to do.

[The letter then expresses amazement at a report from the Divisional Road Engineer's department, presented to the Traffic Policy Committee on Monday 16 January.]

The *Minister has decided* that trunk road improvements *will* be carried out at this point, and that a scheme is included for commitment immediately and requisitioned by April 1967. It is important therefore to accept the invitation issued them under form T.R. 100A (to prepare details and estimates for a *dual carriageway*). Otherwise we shall have to consider alternative arrangements. . . . I earnestly hope that you will undertake this work and forward the layout plan and the T.R. 100B not later than 18 January 1967, so that the scheme may proceed and *I can honour my undertaking to the Vice-Chancellor of the University* that I would be undertaking this work in the immediate future, to assist in the safe passage of students from Warwick University across the trunk road.

Chairmanship of the Planning and Development Committee of Coventry Corporation places some responsibility on me to promote and support the views and resolve of the Council about the Development Plan. . . . Do local authorities count any more? Is local democratic sentiment to be trodden down, and where does the statutory planning function come in? These are not wild sentiments, they have been gelled in the discussion at Liaison Committee level, and you must be aware how much both the County Council and Coventry City Council feel about the road developments in the vicinity of the University and the possibility of injury to the high amenity of Kenilworth Road.

Planning authorities are becoming apprehensive as to the extent to which the roads, be they trunk or urban, will dominate the physical scene, unless great care is taken to ensure suitable landscaping. Kenilworth Road forms one of the finest approaches to any city in the country. It depends for its character on the scale of the road, the height of the trees and the width of the grass verges. It is a heritage of fine landscape architecture we cannot let go without a challenge.

The simple fact is that there is an alternative in planning design to give students the protection required; there is also a purpose to preserve. At one time I said publicly that 'I would give my right arm to preserve the Coventry end of Kenilworth–Warwick Road', and I would give my body to protect the physical scene at Gibbet Hill.

The whole story makes me wonder whether membership of the 'Liaison Committee' is worthless and meaningless. Whether faith in one another, public morality, trust and confidence, and the proper use of the English language mean anything. Two and two don't make four any more, there are not thirty-six inches to the yard and you can drive both ways on any side of the road.

Yours
G. E. Hodgkinson

Chapter 7
Highly Confidential: A Personal Comment by the Editor

I have tried, three or four times, to write a contribution to this book which respects the impersonal tone proper to the 'alliance' of differing views which has made up the 'Warwick movement'. Each time I have come up with muffled rhetoric, which has evaded critical questions – of academic freedom, of university government, and of the rights and wrongs of breaking into files – as to which there are differing emphases within the Warwick movement and among the contributors to this book.

It seems therefore to be more honest to offer an individual comment, using an editor's privilege to give a personal answer to several of these questions: an answer with which other contributors and actors might well disagree.

First, the Warwick 'alliance'. There have been at Warwick, not one, but at least two overlapping circles of conflict which have come to a coincidence in the present crisis. One has been a straightforward struggle to enforce due process – the honest and open operation of democratic procedures of academic self-government – as against undue influence, or manipulation, or the introduction of inappropriate managerial methods. This struggle to uphold the traditional rules of the academic game has been without political overtones. Conservatives have fought as staunchly for the rules as have socialists, and some administrators have fought rather more staunchly than most academics. The staff have obviously been more involved in its episodes than the students, although the latter were driven through every one of its hoops during the Union Building saga, and they understand its significance very well.

The second area of conflict is the one in which students have been pre-eminently involved, and partakes of the international movement of student 'militancy' and revolt. It shares its demands for student control over the student social environment, greater student participation at all levels of decision-making (and also greater participation by non-professorial academic staff), and it has perhaps added to these familiar demands a new seriousness of intention in exploring new modes of relationship between the academic and the civil communities. While some conservatives have taken an active part in this struggle, the leadership has come most often from socialist or radical students; and the academic staff generally have been hesitant in giving their support.

There has been a large area where these two circles of conflict have intersected, and within that area the Warwick alliance has been firm. But at the left and right extremities of each circle there has been a continuous flow of criticism, threatening to erode and – in any moment of distrust – to destroy the alliance altogether. One way of examining the issues involved might be to examine these criticisms.

To the left – in the columns of the *Red Mole*, the *Workers Press* and the fly-sheets of associated sects – there has been a continuous natter of uncomradely narking, directed against Warwick radicals and socialists alike, for their sycophantic compromises with 'liberalism'. Warwick's Open Week failed to set up a revolutionary soviet of workers and students, but was a mere celebration of 'hippiedom'. 'The leadership of the struggle fell into the hands of the liberals. . . . The current wave of struggles about files may have begun at Warwick, but Warwick is no longer in the vanguard of the struggle' (*Redbrick*, 4 March 1970). (But Warwick's struggle has been about a great deal more than files.) So far from moving forward towards outright revolutionary confrontation, the Warwick movement has reinforced the illusions of liberalism, and attempted to turn the wheel of 'history' backwards. Warwick, in this view, is in no sense a peculiar case: it is a typical capitalist university. Translating a simplistic class-struggle model from industry to education, academic staff and 'the Administration' are seen together as one reactionary blur. That blur must be opposed by relentless revolutionary opposition – confrontation after confrontation – until at last the mask of liberalism slips and it reveals its true oppressive features. No alliance is possible, although the odd university teacher may be saved by crossing to the side of the students and giving instant allegiance to whatever they – or the local red mole –

may demand. Any attempt to make the University a better place to live and work in, or to strengthen its liberal defences, is simply to contribute to the mask of illusion.

This kind of analysis – while commencing with the very real dilemma of the limits of change possible in any institution whose financing and government are ultimately determined by capitalist power – proceeds swiftly to polemical abstractions by underestimating the human and constitutional defences which exist – or which can be established – against this power. And the polemic is given a passionate edge by the genuine need to express solidarity with a zestful and courageous American radical student movement which (it is not clearly enough understood) operates within a very different culture, with different educational institutions, and with a sensibility seared by the absolutes of racial conflict and of direct, daily opposition to the Vietnam war.

I am willing to argue elsewhere (as I have done in the past) my disagreements with the nostrums of Instant Student Power. It is more relevant here to argue the case in terms of two of the incidents of the Warwick events – the affair of 42 High Street, Kenilworth, and the question of political files.

At a casual reading, the 42 High Street, Kenilworth, affair (see pages 112–19) appears as a storm in a teacup. Three students gave out leaflets at a girls' High School, giving this address as a meeting-place for the Schools Action Union. In the ensuing correspondence (in which the *wrong* three students were named) the Clerk to the Warwickshire County Council, two MPs, the Warwickshire County Education Officer, the Chairman of the Warwickshire Education Committee and the Vice-Chancellor all took part. The Vice-Chancellor replied to Alderman Douty that he had 'by law no further influence over the outside activities of his students than the Managing Director of Rootes has over the outside activities of his employees', which was, perhaps, a rather more proper reply than his ensuing assurance that 'if I can see an opportunity for taking action you may be sure I will do so'. At the weekly meeting of the University's Officers the matter was discussed further: the Assistant Vice-Chancellor was detailed to 'talk to police about 42 High Street'; and it was suggested that graduate applicants from Essex 'might be carefully screened in future'.

It is worth noting that, in the view of another outsider to the University, this furore among County and University officials about a leaflet was 'a squalid affair'. In a statement to the Press Mr Thomas Litterick, Chairman of the Kenilworth Labour Party, asked:

'What was this propaganda that Councillor Forsyth [and] Alderman Doughty ... think is so subsersive?' The leaflet advocated higher pay for teachers, support for the teachers' strike, higher educational expenditure, abolition of corporal punishment in schools, smaller classes, freedom of choice in matters of dress, hair styles, etc.... 'In revealing the details of this squalid affair the students of Warwick University have performed a public service which deserves the gratitude of the community' (*Coventry Evening Telegraph*, 9 March 1970).

One must thank Mr Litterick for his forthright statement and for his sense of proportion. What should give rise to further concern is the speculation as to what might have happened to any of the (wrongly identified) students if any of them had been dependent upon the Warwickshire education authority for their grant. There has been increasing pressure over the past two years from several quarters (including, alas, a few police-minded administrators and academics) to use the local education authority grants as a means of discipline. Ill-informed laymen have suggested that universities should 'report' militant or refractory students to their LEAs, who could then, on an adverse report, terminate their grants. (We have already noted (p. 37) that Mr Gilbert Hunt suggested on Warwick University's Council that students demonstrating at a Rootes factory might be 'reported' to their LEAs.

This is a problem specific to the British context. Neither the students at the Sorbonne nor those at Berkeley share to the same degree the advantages or the difficulties of the British students' dependence on public grants. In these circumstances the disciplinary procedures of a university assume (like its examination procedures) a quasi-judicial significance, since upon them the reputation and financial-security of the students depend. Any attempt to short-circuit due process, and to vest in senior administrators or professors powers to issue adverse reports to LEAs, would constitute the most severe limitation of student rights, and would affect most punitively students from working-class or lower-income homes.

No responsible university teacher, and very few students, would propose that students should be immune from all disciplinary procedures of an academic character. Apart from qualifying examinations, Warwick – in common with other universities – has procedures by which the odd student who for no good reason is simply failing to do his academic work can be reported to an academic committee (the School of Studies) and (after warning, and with right of representation and appeal) be sent down.

Seen in this context, the 'law and order' lobby set a-buzzing and a-fuzzing by a leaflet could be judged to be a lobby for the suspension of law and for the provocation of disorder. (Students would most certainly 'sit-in' if their fellows were disciplined for exercising their civil rights, and they would be a hundred per cent right to do so.) And any defence by the University's Officers that, first, they did nothing and, second, they merely handled public relations with influential local officials in tactful ways, turns out to be less than convincing. To plan to 'screen' applicants from another university (presumably on some other grounds than academic merit), to assure outsiders that the University authorities will watch for an opportunity 'for taking action', to wonder whether further inquiries in Coventry would be worth while, and to 'talk to' the police – all this is doing *something*. This is to go regrettably beyond the limits of showing tact to local County officials. It is to suggest an identity of interests and of outlook as between County authorities, Conservative MPs and police, together with the University's Officers, on the one hand, as against ill-disciplined university teachers and students on the other.* The Officers of a university that was fully intent to establish,

*Three months after this incident – and after so much talking to officials and police – the University's Officers had still not found time to notify one graduate student's Head of Department (and Supervisor) of the incident, or of what all the talking had been about.

against improper pressure, the prerogatives and independence of their institution as a centre of learning, would have dealt with these inquiries in a very different tone.

It may be argued that, if something was done, nothing *much* was done. This may be true. But the complacent should recall that these incidents should be examined, in a period of particular sensitivity, in the light of a jockeying for positions from which (if uncontested) a great deal might be done. As the County Education Officer informed the Clerk to the County Council: 'the University authorities are placed in a difficult position if, as it seems, the students have not placed themselves within the reach of formal disciplinary measures.' In plain English the (wrongly identified) students had done nothing wrong at all. And, further, the University has constitutional procedures which administrators and university teachers – as well as students – will ensure are fully respected.

It is here that red moles and Maoists, looking down at our contemptible liberal maunderings from the revolutionary heights of North London, tend to go wrong. In so far as they persuade students that *all* the rules, the democratic and constitutional defences, of the institution are no more than liberal 'masks', their analysis could be self-fulfilling. But it is scarcely likely that the students' economic lifeline – the LEA grant – can be defended simply by the tactics of 'confrontation' alone. Once that lifeline is easy to cut, once it becomes possible in any university for students to be disciplined through the LEAs after merely perfunctory proceedings, then the students' world will become one of general insecurity.

In this critical area of conflict, then, militant students would be very unwise to reject out of hand the arguments of liberal constitutionalism; and if, even in this limited area, they are to accept in good faith the alliance of constitutionalists, then their own participation must evince a more than tactical commitment. To stand aside from these procedures, denouncing as bureaucrats and lackeys any students who take part in them, is not a convincing position, politically or morally, from which to defend these procedures if they come – as they may well do in the next two or three years – under heavy attack.

Some of the same argument is true of the most sensitive

issue of all, that of 'political files'. The speed with which the agitation to 'open the files' spread through other universities recalled a *grand peur*. Like all such infectious social fears, it revealed not so much an accumulation of hard particular evidence (I don't myself believe that the more obnoxious items in the Warwick files are 'typical', although such items might be found in a few other places) as a general condition of insecurity and lack of confidence.

Plenty of words have been written already about the difficulties of working out effective procedures to prevent institutions from holding or passing on this kind of information. (No doubt those devices which have been worked out at various places to enable students directly or by proxy to inspect their files are all to the good.) But if one or more powerful University Officer is determined to accumulate such material, he will find ways of doing it – not necessarily on the campus, and certainly not in the ordinary student record files.

In the end, there can be only one effective defence against the holding or use of such extraneous political information: and this, quite simply, must be that it is an outrage to universities and to public opinion to do so. Not only this – opinion must lead swiftly to action, so that offenders, if found out, must be made to know that such behaviour is intolerable.

A climate of opinion must exist within which any informer, however influential he may be, may expect to be shown, metaphorically, off the university's premises (rather than being asked to inform on 'further instances'); in which any student, or administrator, or university teacher, or filing clerk, who has evidence of the collection or use of this kind of material, or any liberal-minded employer who receives irrelevant political information in a reference, can take this instantly before public opinion, and call the author to account. In this way, those who might attempt to build up a security system will be conscious of being surrounded by the far wider counter-security of democracy.

But, if this is true, once again our red moles can't have it both ways: they can't denounce democracy as a spoof and at the same time help to man its defences. I believe that the challenge is, indeed, serious and that the managed corporate society is at

many points closing in. But it hasn't closed in altogether, nor is
the British campus identical with its American counterpart, nor
is there any historical inevitability by which it must become so.
It would be tragic if a section of the Left, through a liking for
large polemical absolutes, through an inattention to the close
detail of political actuality, and perhaps through an emotional
preference for the drama of absolute confrontation, hastened
its own immolation.

To our left the scolding of the Pharisees. But to our right the
enormous pomp and propriety of the self-important academic.
Coming to Warwick from seventeen years of extra-mural
teaching, I have never ceased to be astounded when observing
the preening and mating habits of fully grown specimens of
the species *Academicus Superciliosus*.
  The behaviour patterns of one of the true members of the
species are unmistakable. He is inflated with self-esteem and
perpetually self-congratulatory as to the high vocation of the
university teacher; but he knows almost nothing about any
other vocation, and he will lie down and let himself be walked
over if anyone enters from the outer world who has money or
power or even a tough line in realist talk. He is a consummate
politician in university committees and can scull over every
inch of his own duckpond; but – apart from one or two
distant landmarks, such as the UGC or the SSRC, which
stand like windmills on the horizon – he knows next to nothing
of the world outside his own farmyard. (*Academici Superciliosi*
are never able to see beyond their next meeting, and are continually overcome with amazement and indignation when un-
invited intruders – public opinion, the Press, local political
movements – interpolate themselves upon the agenda.) *Superciliosus* is the most divisible and rulable creature in this country,
being so intent upon crafty calculations of short-term advantages – this favour for his department, that chance of promotion – or upon rolling the log of a colleague who, next week
at the next committee, has promised to roll a log for *him*, that
he has never even tried to imagine the wood out of which all
this timber rolls. He can scurry furiously and self-importantly
around in his committees, like a white mouse running in a

wheel, while his master is carrying him, cage and all, to be sold at the local pet-shop.

These people annoy me a good deal more than do red moles. Academic freedom is for ever on their lips, and is forever disregarded in their actions. They are the last people to whom it can be safely entrusted, since the present moment is never the opportune moment to stand and fight. Show them the last ditch for the defence of liberty, and they will walk backwards into the sea, complaining that the ditch is very ill dug, that they cannot possibly be asked to defend it alongside such a ragged and seditious-looking set of fellows, and, in any case, it would surely be better to write out a tactful remonstrance and present it, on inscribed vellum, to the enemy?

The one unmistakable means of identification of *Academicus Superciliosus* is that he over-reacts to *any* sign of student self-activity. Even a polite deputation or petition throws him into a tizzy. His life is lived in a kind of Awe of Propriety. Whatever the students or the younger staff do is wrong, since it is always embarrassing him in some delicate tactical manoeuvre on a higher committee. If he disagrees with student demands he will not go and argue it out with them, face to face, in a rational way, but he will thumb through old Senate minutes and utter a low disciplinary hiss. He encourages an atmosphere of institutional loyalty, which would have astonished the undergraduates of fourteenth-century Oxford or of eighteenth-century Cambridge, in which it appears as somehow sensational and 'disloyal' for any member of staff to voice publicly at a student meeting criticisms of the university's policies – or, even, sharply expressed intellectual disagreements. Hence the students are defrauded of some of the essential intellectual dialectic from which their own orientations should be worked out. Above all, any serious episode of student 'unrest' – a sit-in, a rough music, or a heckling – is received, with lowered voices, as if it were some aboriginal calamity.

We may leave him there, walking backwards into the sea to his final academically reputable 'glug glug glug' as the waves cover his liberal brow. But those who are genuinely bemused by his arguments should take a steady view of one (perhaps unpalatable) fact in the Warwick events. The academic staff, all of us, throughout the early history of the University, were struck by a paralysis of will – not on this or that local issue, but in any general exertion of control over their own institution. Since the Tyzack Report was marked 'Strictly Confidential' no staff, except for senators, were involved in the decisions as to the major restructuring of the University organization. No attempt was made to involve other members of the University in matters which were their legitimate concern. No inquiry was instituted into the resignation of the Registrar and of his Deputy. None of us instituted any systematic examination or critique of the University's structure and policies, or initiated any proposals for the reconstruction of its Council. Profound and multiplying dissatisfactions, instead of being channelled in any open and constructive direction, ran away in personal resignations, committee warfare and running inter-departmental feuds. The event which ended this paralysis, which at last prised the whole situation open and enabled a constructive critique to be started, was student 'revolt'.

I am not, among my students or acquaintances, notorious for my uncritical admiration of 'youth'. I have been known to lament that young people do not serve for a term in a really well-disciplined organization, such as an Officers' Training Corps or the British Communist Party. Youth, if left to its own devices, tends to become very hairy, to lie in bed till lunch-time, to miss seminars, to be more concerned with the style than with the consequence of actions, and to commit various sins of self-righteous political purism and intellectual arrogance which may be itemized in some other book. In short, I am disposed to admire youth only if, by their actions, they command admiration. As, in the case of the students of Warwick, they most emphatically have.

All students share certain qualities of 'negativity' which, at the simplest level, are an important corrective within university structures. They tend to be concerned with university 'politics' at a primary level of principle and not at a secondary level of interest. Their mere presence on an academic committee or Senate often induces a more dignified and principled conduct on the part of their seniors. Since they have few logs of their own to roll they are not amused when they are spectators of log-rolling. They are not at university to intrigue for 'Chairs'. They generally know much more about the university's actual product – the quality of its teaching – than the university teachers who plan the courses but who scarcely ever enter each others' seminars or lectures.

This goes, so far, for all students. The students of Warwick have added to this many other, positive, qualities. Ever since 11 February they have shown the capacity – not just to give one spirited but impatient heave to the system – but to take the leading part in a long, complex, tactically intricate running conflict. They have resisted all tendencies to divide into sectarian groupings. They have maintained their early positions of principle, and have not given way before special pleading, or been discouraged by inadequate support from the staff. They have shown patience and growing maturity in learning to adjust their strategy to the slower-moving modes of extra-University opinion.

'Aha!' says *Academicus Superciliosus*, struggling back out of the sea, an almost-militant glint in his eye, 'so you condone illegal actions, damage to property, the breaking-open of files, the theft of private and confidential correspondence?' I am fairly caught by the question, which I have evaded for weeks under the formula: 'Without making any judgement as to the propriety of . . .'. That formula is fair enough for people on the periphery of the conflict. But since I have argued that only student revolt laid open issues of grave public concern, and since it is evident that these issues would scarcely have become clear without the aid of documents thus brought to light, can I evade an answer any longer?

Clearly I must and do support this action of the Warwick students also. I support it as an action which, like all actions, exists not as an abstract generality but as a specific action in a specific context. Most English democrats supported the demonstrators for the Second Reform Bill who tore down the Hyde Park railings in 1866. No one supposed that this necessarily entailed support for the tearing-down of all railings at all other parks. Only a really subtle and unworldly academic mind could suppose that support for Warwick students who, after coming upon the 'Montgomery documents', took a deliberate decision to proceed to the examination of other files, thereby must entail support for any and every other raid on files. Such raids could be motivated by hysteria or by uninformed curiosity; they would have a similar political and moral content only if the files had been giving out a similar unwholesome smell.

I must confess also that, as a historian, I find a certain piquancy in that moment. It is my trade to open files, but the authors of the correspondence have always been long dead. One of the difficulties in writing 'contemporary history' is that, until the files have been opened, the actual thoughts and motives of the actors may be difficult to determine because of their public image. But here, for a moment, the actuality and the image co-existed, giving a sense of double vision; and even when the inertia of institutional routine reasserted itself, there lingered the sense of a new dimension to its reality – what the institution wished to be taken for set alongside one's new knowledge of what it actually was.

Of *course* no correspondent likes the idea of militant youth going through his confidential letters: certainly no bad-tempered, middle-aged correspondent like myself. (I was later told that one file which attracted a good deal of sardonic interest was a bulky file full of my own fatuous and long-winded attempts at resignation.) What made the candid eyes of some first-year students blink was not so much the Catchpole report and suchlike but the revelation of the stark old Adam which their seniors and mentors usually disguise beneath their lecturing habit – the waspish notes and back-biting memoranda of that adult world. Well, *Superciliosus*, I agree that it was not altogether *nice*; but if you can't also see that the scene had its own bitter humour – and a humour very properly aimed against you and me – then you are lacking in some sense of proportion.

And, finally, on the matter of files. The students, having taken that decision, executed it responsibly. They published nothing which was not, in their view, of public significance. Whatever personal matters they may have stumbled upon they suppressed. The occupation was not succeeded by a wave of irrelevant personal gossip. But for some days afterwards, as they looked at all of us on the staff, there was something hard in their eyes.

At Warwick we are now awaiting the report of Lord Radcliffe's inquiry. The reasons why the students and a number of the staff have rejected this inquiry, and continue to call for a public inquiry instead, are very simple. They do not call in question Lord Radcliffe's eminence or his high qualifications. But they are bound to ask whether Lord Radcliffe, as Chancellor of the University into which he is inquiring, can really be seen to be uninfluenced by the concern that his institution should stand well in public opinion. His difficulties are made greater by the fact that he knows personally, has dined with and been on Christian name terms with, some of the University's Council members and Officers, whereas the greater part of the staff and perhaps all of the students are not known to him at all. He will, no doubt, make allowance for this kind of influence, but further difficulties remain. A private inquiry of this kind has no power to subpoena witnesses, nor to examine them under oath. And, as William Wilson, MP for Coventry South, has pointed out (*Coventry Evening Telegraph*, 16 March 1970), it will be confined strictly to University matters and will not extend to the use of 'agents' in the Coventry Labour Party's rooms, or other extra-University matters.

It would be especially unfortunate if Lord Radcliffe should take a decision to separate in his Report the indivisible issues of the 'political files' and of 'improper administrative conduct within the University'. For, as all historians know, no evidence can be fully understood until it is placed in its context. In a situation in which the evidence brought to light may give only a very partial view of evidence still undisclosed (as pencilled filing annotations show, certain documents were held, not in the Registry at all, but in the Vice-Chancellor's lodge*), then the general issues of confidence and of due administrative process become of the first relevance in interpreting the evidence

---

*To which Mr Gilbert Hunt sent one of his pieces of information (see p. 110).

disclosed. In the absence of evidence bearing upon the whole question of confidence, it is scarcely possible to be satisfied as to whether or not this or that isolated piece of evidence was or was not 'unsolicited', and as to whether its receipt did or did not influence any University decision.

Thus the students are likely to continue to press for a public inquiry, for which there is growing public support. Beyond this, the Warwick movement faces the classical dilemma of a reform movement which has access to no constitutional means to enforce reform. We face the Unreconstituted Council in the same manner as the British people faced, in 1831, the Unreformed House of Commons. The logic of the whole conflict leads not just to a defensive position (of establishing traditional safeguards for 'academic freedom'), but must lead on to a positive and far-reaching reconstruction of the University's self-government and of its relations to the community. We have forced matters to a point where we must demand a *more* democratic constitution than any existing university enjoys, or nothing – and perhaps something very much worse than nothing – will have been won.

This means, first, that – if it should be shown upon inquiry that any University Officers or Council members have acted improperly – they should be clearly and openly called to account and, if necessary, replaced. It is extraordinary the way in which the Establishment resists any such procedure, in a country which proffers itself as a democratic model. Not only the 'law and order' brigade, who thirst for the disciplining of students, but also our friend *Superciliosus*, throws up his hands in horror at the mere suggestion of open democratic accountability. In England 'we' have better ways of conducting such affairs; if 'mistakes' have been made, then in three years, or perhaps even in two, certain changes may be made, provided that they are made discreetly. Above all, they must not appear to be made in response to popular – still less *student!* – pressure; indeed, a pre-condition of any change is that the institution shall first, at whatever cost, be restored to discipline. Any alternative would threaten the position of every university administration in the Free Democratic World.

In this kind of way certain senior members of the University, themselves perhaps a little compromised by the 'mistakes', who have themselves offered absolutely nothing and risked absolutely nothing in the conflict, arrange among each other its outcome, in ways which will effect the least possible change but may enhance their own power.

In such ways the elders of the academic – and of other – establishments indicate the true value which they set upon democracy. And if they succeed in handling matters in their own established way, then of course the red moles and Maoists will have got the better of the argument with us. The liberal tradition *will* have turned out to be a slipping mask, public opinion *will* have turned out to have offered no safeguard against 'political files', the corporate society will have moved a step closer – not only at Warwick but at every university in the country – and the whole texture of democratic life will be a little thinner.

The second objective of the Warwick movement is for a reconstitution of the University's government. Committees are now studying – and discussions are proceeding with people in the local community – with a view to working out a new democratic charter. While such a charter should enlarge the representation of both staff and students, no one has argued that a university should be wholly self-governing, without responsibility to the society within which it is situated. Clearly, a university can't grow in any direction it chooses, without regard to social needs and demands; and clearly, also, relationships with the community – with industry at every level, with the Shakespeare Memorial and Belgrade Theatres, with local teachers and welfare workers, with ordinary citizens, perhaps even with pupils at Kenilworth's Abbey High School – can only enrich the University's life and help to dig students and staff out of their somewhat introverted isolation.

How to achieve such links requires the most careful study. There are simple technical problems – in what ways are lay members to be co-opted or appointed? To supplement so many industrialists with so many nominees of the organized trade-union movement would only be to offer some formal satisfaction of a 'party-political' kind. (The trouble, in any case, with the appointment of nominees from outside institutions is that it generally gives rise to the nomination of persons so important and so busy with other public duties that they can't give more than a casual formal interest to the University's affairs.) It was not a militant student but a spokesman of the Coventry Labour Party, Councillor N. P. Lister, who proposed in the City Council chamber that representatives might be directly elected from the workshop floor:

In the population there must be a worker, a trade unionist, or a housewife of a working family, who has something to offer to the University. It is in this spirit that we feel we can contribute more (*Coventry Evening Telegraph*, 11 March 1970).

It is in the same spirit that Warwick students are exploring a new charter.

One sees, fairly frequently, splenetic letters in the correspondence columns, arguing that students, who are dependent upon public money, should be subject to public controls. In so far as this is true, it is true equally of Vice-Chancellors and (as we have argued sufficiently in this book) for universities as a whole. But if 'public opinion' is exerted by too direct means, then – as American experience shows – the university can be thrown into the arena of 'party-political' warfare in some of its most philistine forms. As Professor Harold Perkin noted (*The Times Literary Supplement*, 19 March 1970):

Universities are at once detached from and embedded in the life of society. As centres of inquiry and criticism they must stand apart from the rest of society, detach themselves from too much dependence on it, so as to be free to follow uncomfortable and unpalatable truths wherever they may lead....

It is a question of adjusting the proper area of an institution's self-determination and control by its own members in relation to that proper area in which society's own demands and needs can be indicated. But, once we have reached this point, the argument becomes infinitely more complex, because there is not, of course, in Britain *one* 'public', but many different publics, with different demands, needs and values. Hence, to respond to social demands does not mean to respond instantaneously to one particular indicator of demands – government policy or the policies of senior industrialists – but to take part, at many different levels in society, in the argument between differing indices of social priority. A university must leave itself the freedom actively to seek out social needs which have not, as yet, percolated to the level of government or which may not coincide with the needs of industrialists; and if links are to be forged there is also a need (as one Warwick student argued) for links to be made between 'the subversives in the University and the subversives in society'.

What is at issue here is not just the government of one university, but the whole way in which a society selects its priorities and orders itself. I suppose I am the only one of the contributors to this book who can recall, as an adult experience, the international symbol which Coventry became in the war; and who took part in the brief episode of optimistic socialist populism, between 1944 and 1947, when there really was abroad an intention to re-build cities and to re-order industries according to the democracy of need. It is an irony that Coventry, with its energetic labour movement, its brave new comprehensive schools, its famous cathedral, its planned industrial belt, should have become host, within its City boundaries, to a University which could be taken as a symbol of an altogether alien order.

That order supposes that – whatever governments may come and go – the summation of social good may be achieved by one thing only: the greater stability of the ongoing industrial system. Since this is so, then clearly the industrial managers and their financial advisers are the men who must stand at the top. Their contribution to 'society', and their 'advice', must be overwhelmingly more important and more realistic than the contribution or advice of a musician, or of a probation officer, or of a primary-school teacher. Government also should indicate in every way the educational priority of 'industry' and of 'business'; and by far the most important educational products of a university must be those which go to reinforce a system which in fact is directed by criteria of profitability, although the public image is of efficiency and economic growth. Supplementing this ever-present, persuasive propaganda of priorities, there come new methods of management, a new insistence upon the subjugation of the individual to institutional loyalties. The demands of the institution become larger – moving outwards from the working life to the private and social life of its employees – and its attempts to enforce loyalties by moral or disciplinary means, by streaming its procedures or by managing promotions and career prospects, become greater. The managers, at the top, need not even see themselves as police-minded men; they think they are acting in the interests of greater 'efficiency'; any other course would damage the institution's 'public image' or would encourage subversion.

Unfortunately, inside the institution the workers work to rule and the 'long-haired louts wearing jeans and sandals' lounge against the walls. So that, instead of 'efficiency', the managers drive headlong towards confrontation after confrontation. Because neither efficiency nor productivity were ever, in the long run, achieved by the manipulation of people, by limiting their rights, by defrauding them of their own initiatives, by denying to them participation in the control of their own affairs.

And what is wrong, again, is the whole system of values – the entire ordering of human priorities – of this insistent managerial propaganda. It is sad to see even the scholars themselves hesitate in their work and wonder about the *use* of what they are doing. Even they begin to feel, defensively, that a salesman or an advertising executive is perhaps a more important and productive human being than an actor, or a designer, or a teacher of English. Able and perhaps eminent men in their own disciplines, they capitulate without a struggle before the intellectually specious proposal that a university can train young men and women, who have no industrial experience, in a 'managerial science' in which they master no single academic skill – whether as economists or engineers or sociologists – but which will miraculously equip them to 'manage' the affairs of the skilled workers and technicians of Britain. Step by step the defensive scholar resigns his wider allegiances – to a national or international discourse of ideas – and retreats within the limited area of manoeuvre allotted to him within the managerial structure. Step by step he resigns his responsibility, not only to listen selectively for social demands, but to insert *into* society the demand for priorities which it is his own first

duty to make: that man exists and progresses, not only by productive technology, but also by the strength of his ideas and by
the artefacts of his culture. In his submission to a subordinate
role in a managerial system, he is re-enacting the meaning, for
Britain in the 1970s, of the *trahison des clercs.*

So, against all this, we have raised at Warwick, not only a
new flag or two, but some very ancient and tattered flags, even
older than those of rotten liberalism. We also have our allegiances: the very pressures of this new institutionally centred
society make for peculiarly intense institutional conflicts, peculiarly obsessive internal confrontations. We apologize to
readers for our obsessions. But the outcome of our conflict concerns them also. It will decide not only whether this University
can become a good, technologically well-equipped and intellectually alert, self-governing community – as it still, despite
all its history, could be – or whether it will become simply 'the
Business University' from which all other aspirations fall
rapidly away. The outcome of this episode will also be some
kind of an index of the vitality of democratic process – and of
the shape of the next British future.

General Conclusion

The examination of the University files during the student occupation of the Registry at Warwick was a political action whose repercussions have spread outwards from the University to other universities, and to the wider society of which they are a part. We have had neither the time nor the information to examine all these repercussions.

At William Ellis School the headmaster (who had sent the report on Michael Wolf) was forced to justify his action to angry pupils and parents; and school pupils around the country were again made aware of the power that lies in the hands of headmasters. At more than a dozen universities agitations began on the issue of 'political files', and university authorities, under pressure, gave assurances as to the character of student records. The publication by members of Birmingham University of a well-edited selection of documents (from the Warwick files) received by Butterworth in his capacity as Chairman of the Inter-University Council, and relating to the Medical School of University College, Rhodesia, revealed the imposition by the Smith regime of intolerable racist conditions upon the work of the new teaching hospital in Salisbury. Following these revelations – and the indignation aroused by them among students and faculty members of the Birmingham Medical School – the Senate of Birmingham University has decided to phase out its links with University College, Rhodesia.

Thus the 'Warwick Affair' has raised the general issue of the role of universities within contemporary society. This book does not describe an episode in local history; the writing of it is itself a political act, one of the series which were set in motion on 11 February, and whose outcome is yet to be enacted. These events have given more relevance and importance than ever before in Britain to the international conflict as to the role of a university in a modern capitalist society.

United as we are in opposition to what is in our opinion an industrial–intellectual oligarchy as described in this book, we can still be sharply divided in our response to the underlying questions. Is it inevitable that the university will be reduced to the function of providing, with increasingly authoritarian efficiency, pre-packed intellectual commodities which meet the requirements of management? Or can we by our efforts transform it into a centre of free discussion and action, tolerating and even encouraging 'subversive' thought and activity, for a dynamic renewal of the whole society within which it operates? Can we achieve anything by working through the existing social and political institutions – academic, national and local governmental – or are these institutions themselves too deeply compromised? Can we change, in radical ways, the structures of the university and its links with the community, or will the universities see themselves destroyed rather than have such changes allowed? Would any partial success achieved in such a struggle be bound to be self-defeating (without far-reaching changes in the society itself) as institutions re-grouped and absorbed our gains within a new and more subtle system of discipline and direction?

At Warwick as elsewhere there have been widely different, more or less well thought-out answers to these questions; and different answers have resulted in different emphases upon the kinds of action which can, with most effect, be taken. And, equally, there have been different assessments – to which this book bears witness – as to the effectiveness of these actions. We invite our readers to join in these arguments and to support whichever of these kinds of action they judge to be most effective. For, in all its forms, the movement goes on.

Index